THE EPISCOPATE AND THE PRIMACY

ABOUT THE BOOK

It is widely expected that the Second Vatican Council will complete the work of the Ecumenical Council of 1870, and supplement the definition of Papal primacy and infallibility by a theological clarification of the meaning of the episcopal office. In his speculative study Father Rahner shows that the bishop is not only the Pope's delegate, but that he exercises his office in a particular place as the representative of the Universal Church, and of the "College of Apostles", to which Christ entrusted the government of the Church. Defining the essence of the Church as the historical continuation of the Word of God made flesh, Father Rahner sees, in the present-day diocese, in the "Local Church", not so much an administrative subdivision of the Universal Church, but the very concentration of the Church in her actuality, expressed in the celebration of the Eucharist. Supported by Father Ratzinger's outline of the Church's traditional teaching on primacy and episcopacy, Father Rahner is able to shed new light on the nature of the episcopal office, its purpose and functions in the Church and in the world today.

QUAESTIONES DISPUTATAE

KARL RAHNER
JOSEPH RATZINGER

THE EPISCOPATE AND
THE PRIMACY

HERDER

FREIBURG

NELSON

EDINBURGH-LONDON

Original edition "Episkopat und Primat", Herder, Freiburg

Translated by Kenneth Barker, Patrick Kerans, Robert Ochs and Richard Strachan

Nihil Obstat: Joannes M. T. Barton, S. T. D., L. S. S.,
Censor deputatus

Imprimatur: † Georgius L. Craven. Vic. Gen. Epus. Sebastopolis
Westmonasterii, die 21ᵃ Augusti, 1962

The Nihil Obstat and Imprimatur are a declaration that a book or pamphlet is considered to be free from doctrinal or moral error. It is not implied that those who have granted the Nihil Obstat and Imprimatur agree with the contents, opinions or statements expressed.

Library of Congress Catalog Card Number: 62-19565

First published in West Germany © 1962 Herder KG

Printed in West Germany by Herder

Eminentissimo et Excellentissimo Domino

Domino Julio Döpfner

S. R. E. Presbytero Cardinali et Episcopo Berolinensi
Sacræ Theologiæ Doctori
hoc qualecumque opusculum auctores d. d. d.

CONTENTS

FOREWORD

Both the coming Council and its expected agenda focus attention once again on the importance of the relationship between the episcopate and the primacy. In many important respects this question is truly a *"quaestio disputata"*, and thus definitely falls within the scope of this series. Yet no one will expect to find here an exhaustive treatment of the question, or to encounter in these pages only such views as enjoy universal acceptance.

The first part of this work appeared in Karl Rahner's *Sendung und Gnade* (Innsbruck: Tyrolia Verlag, 1959, pp. 239–262) and with the kind permission of the publisher is reprinted here in order to round off the subject to some extent. The second part appeared originally in *Catholica,* Vol. 13 (1959), pp. 260–277, and is reprinted without change. The third part has not hitherto been published. It is hardly necessary to add that each of the authors is responsible only for his own work.

The authors thank His Eminence, the Most Reverend Julius Cardinal Döpfner, for allowing them to dedicate this volume to him.

Innsbruck and Bonn, January 1961.

Karl Rahner — Joseph Ratzinger

I

THE EPISCOPATE AND THE PRIMACY

Karl Rahner

1. The State of the Question

Is it permissible to feel that we could reflect more on the constitution of the Church than we have hitherto done? Since the
Church and her theology are always aware of her nature,
there is never any question of a leap from downright ignorance
to knowledge, say, like the discovery of Australia, but rather of
a growth in the reflex consciousness of a knowledge which, in
substance, the Church has always possessed, as when, for example,
after a long life of active and candid self-discovery, a person may
additionally also come to know himself with the help of all
available psychological tests and concepts.

Even today, this reflex knowledge of her own, permanent
nature which the Church has, can grow. Deeper insight is
possible not only into the actual mysteries of this Church which
is the community of the faithful in the Spirit of God, the
body of Christ, the beginning of the Kingdom of God, the
primal sacrament of God's eschatological salvation. It can also
embrace her constitution – that is to say, those juridical bonds
which create and sustain her as a "perfect society". Here too, one
may well think, the nature of the Church could be conceived
in clearer and more conscious fashion. For if we consult one of

the current theological textbooks, we learn that the Church has a "hierarchical" structure, in that Christ entrusted to the Apostolic college and to the bishops, the successors of the apostles, the power to preach the gospel, to administer the sacraments, and to give spiritual guidance. We learn that the Church is not a purely voluntary association of a democratic kind, established by men, but one whose fundamental rights, duties and powers were established by God.

We are further told that this hierarchically constituted Church has a "monarchical" summit in the immediate, universal primacy of jurisdiction of Peter and his successors, the popes. But with this the doctrine of the constitution of the Church, insofar as that constitution is of direct divine origin, is exhausted. It would seem to us that the relation between the hierarchic-episcopal and the monarchic–papal structure of the Church – a question which, as we know, the Vatican Council of 1870 was not allowed time to broach – is still not clear. Nor indeed is the one homogeneous nature of this constitution clarified, its ultimate basic idea, by merely affirming these two powers in the Church. A certain obscurity still shrouds the "metaphysics" of the Church's constitution.

When such a problem is raised one can, of course, say that in this matter an answer can hardly be expected beyond the clear and common teaching. After all, it can be argued, the Church is a juridical entity unique in history, instituted by a free disposition of God which cannot be deduced from necessary metaphysical principles, both of which facts – her uniqueness and her foundation through God's free will – render it unlikely that, by means of some sort of supernatural philosophy of law and constitutional metaphysics (which would always proceed from general and neccessary principles), much more could be said than is already explicitly known. One could indeed ask oneself whether there is such a thing as a written constitution of the Church; or, better, wonder that there is none. The Code of Canon Law is, in content, purpose and make-up, not a constitution of the Church, even though it can be said to contain the most important constitutional rules. It might be asked further, whether there could be such a thing as a comprehensive written constitution of the Church on the lines of a modern, written state constitution. But the question cannot be pursued here.

This scepticism may be justified. Those who profess it will certainly not be refuted by the modest observations that follow. The author does not presume to attempt a comprehensive solution to the problem that has been posed, but merely to set forth some tentative considerations prompted by the feeling that we can and should make progress in the theology of this constitution, which is more than a matter of articles. Such considerations may also have a practical import. For although the nature of the Church is of divine origin and indestructible, nevertheless its realization in every-day life, even when under the protection of the promised Holy Ghost, is still exposed to man's freedom, to his whims and to his errors. And therefore this nature can be manifested either to better or to worse effect. A deeper, more conscious knowledge of the Church's nature can also contribute towards the ever purer realization of this nature, even in her most ordinary activities, and it is precisely through this contribution that the Spirit of the Church affords her his own assistance.

We shall try to form a few ideas about the constitution of the

13

Church by comparing it with the constitutions of other societies. This method is perfectly legitimate. For, although we cannot thereby directly contemplate the ultimate mystery of the Church, still she is a visible society with legal powers and a juridical framework which belongs on the one hand to her divinely established essence (therefore not merely to the human law within the Church), and which on the other hand (because they are found within this world, incarnate) lend themselves to comparison with other human legal relationships just as the humanity of Christ can be compared with the nature of other men, because he became "consubstantial" with us.

2. The Constitution of the Church

It is commonly said that the Church has a monarchical constitution. If this is taken to mean that the pope, as an individual, has full, direct, ordinary and general episcopal primacy of jurisdiction over the whole Church and each of her parts and members – including the bishops – then the monarchical constitution of the Church is axiomatic for Catholics.[1] But a monarchical constitution is usually understood to mean an hereditary monarchy and not an elective one, whereas the pope is at least *de facto* elected.[2] This distinction is not insignificant. For where office and sovereign power are hereditary and where, therefore, their subject is designated by biological factors largely independent

[1] Vatican Council; Denzinger *Enchiridion Symbolorum,* no. 1831 (henceforward referred to as "Dz."). CJC, can. 218.
[2] In the present context we cannot decide the question whether this must be so by divine law, or wheter *per se* a pope — since celibacy is only a

14

of the intellectual and moral decisions of men, the state or society in question is more stable and compact than where the bearer of supreme power is ever and again designated by election, *i.e.,* by a free, deliberate act of men themselves. This also holds true where the actual content of power subsists independent of the electors. Even here the *exercise* of this power is deeply influenced by the historical, the elective character of the chosen ruler, and therefore by the character of his electors as well. To define the Church as a monarchy is to fail to throw into relief the scope which, as history shows, here remains for the play of the charismatic and unexpected qualities of the Church's character, her perennial youthfulness, her vigour.

Furthermore, monarchy, when not reduced by an essentially extraneous element into constitutional monarchy, is of its own nature "absolute" monarchy. This need not mean tyranny or totalitarianism. An absolute monarchy may recognize that it is bound to observe the natural law as, for example, the better representatives of eighteenth century absolutism did; it may be enlightened or patriarchal absolutism; it may, because of pressing physical circumstances or by a policy consciously adopted (though not really consistent with the system as such), respect a defined and organically grown social order such as that of estates. Nevertheless, such a monarchy can be absolute to the extent that everything within the bounds of physical possibility and of morality — which can be realized in a given historical

positive church law – could set up the Church as an hereditary monarchy, or himself designate his successor in some other way. Cf. for example, A. Straub, *De Ecclesia Christi* (Innsbruck, 1912) n. 596; J. Salaverri, "De Ecclesia Christi", *Sacrae Theologiae Summa* 1[4] (Madrid, 1958), p. 655, note 41.

15

situation—proceeds from the will of one man and of one man only. Now is the Church a monarchy in this sense? The answer is not easy. Is someone an absolute monarch in the sense defined if he possesses *suprema et plena potestas jurisdictionis vere episcopalis, ordinaria et immediata?*[3] The answer, of course, depends on terminological precisions which are always arbitrary to a certain extent, since they could be expressed differently regardless of the reality or the truth of the objects and propositions under consideration. But if we accept the meaning of an absolute monarchy according to the definition given above, then we must say that the pope is not a monarch[4] of the Church.

The reasons are clear. In an absolute monarchy there are no constitutional authorities beside the monarch, existing independent of the monarch's will. Indeed there may be facts and moral obligations which limit the will of the absolute monarch. But where his will is fundamentally limited by some legally binding reality which, as such, belongs to the constitutional structure of the society and not merely to the moral norms which stand above positive constitutional law, we can no longer speak of an absolute monarchy. But the Church is so constituted. The will of the pope, insofar as he has the highest authority in the Church, is limited by a reality which, according to the very will of God, belongs to the constitution of the Church, namely, the episcopate. Not only is the pope physically unable to abolish the episcopate (since in doing so he would rob himself of the means of administering his government of the universal Church), but he

---

[3] CJC, can. 218.
[4] The Vatican Council and the CJC therefore do not use this concept. When it does appear in theology it is used in a broader sense than that defined here.

also confronts an episcopate which, as such, is not his civil service instituted by himself which he could abolish, at least legally, if not in fact. For the episcopate itself is of divine right.[5] It is only conjoined with this episcopate – as immediately sprung from the institution of Christ as itself – that the papal primacy juridically constitutes the Church.

This does not exclude the pope from being above the individual bishop as an individual, even in his official capacity as bishop. The pope has direct and ordinary jurisdiction over each bishop as well. He determines which person shall possess the powers of a bishop,[6] and according to what is now the common teaching, gives that person his powers.[7] By that very fact it is open to the pope to fix the precise limits of these powers, to extend them, to restrict them by reserving certain elements of these powers to himself, even in principle, although, of their nature, they would fall within the bishop's competence. But it does not follow (quite the contrary) that the episcopate as a whole could be abolished by the pope, that it is only an instru-

---

[5] Cf. the Council of Trent: Dz. 960 and 966; Vatican Council: Dz. 1821 and 1826; CJC, can. 108. Accordingly, Leo XIII in his Encyclical *"Satis Cognitum"* expressly teaches that the bishops are not to be considered as representatives of the Roman pope, since they have their own proper authority; *". . . nec tamen Vicarii Romanorum Pontificum putandi, quia potestatem gerunt sibi propriam . . ."* ASS 28, 1895–96, p. 723; cf. also Dz. 1962. Hence they care for their flocks not in the name of the pope, but in Christ's and their own name, so that they are successors of the apostles by divine decree. Pius XII emphasized both of these points in *"Mystici Corporis"* (AAS 35, 1943, pp. 211 ff.; Dz. 2287). Cf. also Pius XII in his allocution *"Si Diligis"* (AAS 46, 1954, p. 314).

[6] Dz. 968; 1750 ff.; CJC, can. 329, § 2.

[7] Cf. J. Salaverri, *op. cit.*, p. 632, no. 374, where he refers to Pius XII's *"Mystici Corporis"* (AAS 35, 1943, pp. 211 ff.; Dz. 2287) and *"Ad Sinarum*

ment of papal authority, that therefore the bishops are only the pope's officials, who, as his functionaries, are mere executive organs of the one absolute, monarchical power of the pope. As physical persons they receive their authority from the pope. But he does not confer on them a part of his own personal power to be exercised by them in his name. He gives them a power which, as distinct from that of the pope (even though subject to it), must exist in the Church according to the will of Christ himself, and forms one of the constituent elements of the Church and not of the papacy as such.

If it is true that the pope has a universal, supreme and direct episcopal jurisdiction over the whole Church and therefore over the bishops too, then it must be said that the authority of the bishops, whereby they are not mere functionaries of the pope, considered *materially* (that is, in its mere objectivity and through its subordination to the higher jurisdiction of the pope), cannot be separated from papal authority.[8] This means that there is nothing the bishops can do which the pope could not do, and that all they can do they can do in subordination to the pope. There is no

Gentem" (AAS 47, 1955, p. 9). In accordance with what has been said above, in conferring this office the pope does not delegate a part of his own authority to the bishop nominated by him, but grants him a share in that authority of the universal episcopate which Christ has entrusted to the Church. The ability to communicate a power and the ability to exercise the same power when it has not been communicated to another, are obviously not the same thing. Hence we cannot conclude that what the bishop receives is a delegated papal authority, he being thus a mere official of the pope, from the fact that he receives his authority through the pope.

[8] For this reason the Vatican Council uses the concept "episcopal" to describe the pope's authority. Dz. 1827.

doubt that this incontestable position, solemnly taught by the Vatican Council, gave the impression both inside and especially outside the Church, that the bishops are only officials, functionaries of the pope. When, however, it is pointed out that according to the equally definitive common doctrine the episcopate is of divine right, since the Church expressly teaches (Pius IX, Leo XIII, Pius XII) that even *after* the Vatican Council, the bishops are not mere officials of the pope, it still remains difficult to see how the two facts – the universal and direct primacy of jurisdiction of the pope on the one hand, and the divine institution and indissolubility of the episcopate on the other (as an irreducible, if not independent power), – can be reconciled with each other. Because this point remains obscure in practice the notion persists, both inside and outside the Church, that she is an absolute monarchy governed by the pope through his officials, the bishops. Why should we not openly and candidly admit that this unexpressed, but widespread and almost instinctive feeling can have involuntary but not insignificant effects in the life of the Church? One of these effects may be (and here we would pass no judgment on the existence and actual extent of this effect) that the "official" feels that the degree of his responsible initiative is very limited, since as the mere organ of a higher authority he must almost invariably wait for the initiative to come from above. It may be felt that the obscurity of the question we have been discussing could be clarified to better effect than hitherto.

3. Primacy and Episcopate
compared with the Relationship between Universal Church and Local Church

The non-Catholic legal historian who does not believe in the organic development of the Church's constitutional law will say that the doctrine of the divine institution of the episcopate and its peculiar rights and duties is a verbal residue from the time when such was the actual state of affairs in the Catholic Church; that her teaching on the universal and direct papal primacy of jurisdiction even over the bishops, as this has been understood and put into practice since the Vatican Council, cannot in fact be reconciled with the old doctrine, as is shown by usage, by people's feelings and by the admission that there is no legal power of any substance which the bishop could independently exercise in such a way that the pope could not withdraw the exercise of it from him by restricting his authority, or deposing him, or the like.

There are a number of ways in which we can try to shed light upon this obscurity. First of all the question arises: whence comes this remarkable duality, this interlocking of papal and episcopal authority? How can it be made clear that the concept here confronting us is not so involved, so impenetrable, so apparently tortuous as to indicate a merely verbal harmonization of two irreconcilables?

The historical and theological answer to this question seems to lie in the fact that an individual "church" is not just an administrative district of the whole Church, but bears a unique relationship to the universal Church, one based on the nature of the Church and on her differentiation from natural territorial societies. It is in the light of this relationship that the relationship between pope and bishop can be understood and justified. What appeared to be the suspect complexity of this relation now reveals itself as a consequence of the Church's very character as a supernatural mystery.

These statements require elucidation. We could try to answer our question by referring to the apostles and their appointment by Christ as hierarchical leaders of the Church under Peter. Indeed ecclesiology rightly appeals to the foundation of the apostolic college by Christ in order to prove the existence in the Church of the episcopal office and its establishment by Christ, whilst clearly recognizing that the apostles were not simply the first bishops, (since they enjoyed prerogatives which bishops do not have, because they were not local bishops), and that it is not so easy as one would gather from many a textbook to determine whether a monarchical episcopate existed always and everywhere from the very beginning, or whether there was, here and there in the primitive Church, associate government of individual Christian communities, albeit authoritative and proceding from above. If, however, we merely cite the position of Peter and the apostles in the primitive Church in attempting to explain the seemingly remarkable relationship between primacy and episcopate, then we defer the question without answering it. For we still must explain why the other apostles are not reduced to the status of mere administrative organs and representatives of the Petrine authority, if we assign to Peter the same authority according to Scripture that the Vatican dogma predicates of the pope. Therefore we should not in the first instance fall back on the relation between Peter and the apostles, since the bishops, governing

21

as they do a limited territory, differ essentially from the apostles, even from the point of view of jurisdiction, so that it is not at all easy to say to what extent they are "successors" of the apostles, and it is best to understand this expression in the sense that the function of the apostolic college as a whole is continued in the Church primarily by the episcopal college as a whole,[9] and not in the sense that each bishop is the direct successor of a particular apostle, because in that case neither his confinement to one territory nor his more limited teaching power could be plausibly explained.

Therefore, as we were saying, the solution[10] should be sought in the fundamental relation which obtains between the local Church and the universal Church. It has long been acknowledged that this is a unique relation not found between other societies and their parts, at least not in this intensity and with this significance. The layman in these questions will see this most clearly if he remembers that one speaks of the universal Church and of the individual community, even in the New Testament, as the "Church". The Church which Christ redeemed by his blood is the universal Church; but the individual community at a certain place is also the "Church", in Ephesus, for example. This strange way of speaking cannot be explained by saying that the word for the whole is used to designate the part and that there is nothing strange about it. It is as strange as calling London the United Kingdom. Behind this usage lies a conviction and an intuition which are not at all self-explanatory, and which mean something quite different from the truism that a particular community is a member and an administrative district of the universal Church.

[9] We shall deal with this question in Part Three of this book.
[10] To put it more cautiously, a partial solution of the question.

The idea at the root of this usage has a history going back far beyond New Testament times. It is rooted in the problem of pre-Christian Jewish theology as to where that holy people of God, to whom his promises were made, is palpably and conclusively to be found in history, since this same people in the concrete (according to the "flesh") remains recalcitrant to God's decree and unbelieving. The thought naturally arises that, since God's promises and faithfulness cannot come to nought, the "people", "Israel", still truly exists, even if it survives only in a "faithful remnant", in a brotherhood of a few loyal souls. A limited administrative district in one community cannot cause the totality of this community to live on, when the totality as such has disappeared, if the part was nothing more than a part, a mere organ, not endowed with the sensibility and the various faculties of the whole organism. On the other hand, if the whole is so present in the part that it can fully consummate itself there according to its nature, and if the whole cannot by any means disappear while the part still lives, then the part is indeed more than a mere part, and rightly bears the name of the whole. This is exactly how pre-Christian Jewish theology conceived the faithful remnant, the individual community of brethren, in which God was truly served in faith according to his law.

In order to develop this basic thought more systematically we can also say that the Church as a whole, where she becomes "event" in the full sense of the term, is necessarily a local Church. In the local Church the whole Church becomes tangible. Further explanation is needed to show exactly what this means.[11]

---

[11] In the next few paragraphs we repeat the ideas which we developed in *Die Pfarre*, edited by Hugo Rahner, S.J. (Freiburg i. B., 1956).

When asked what is this Church in its entirety, founded by Christ for all men, the answer we, as men of today, instinctively turn to is a "perfect society", an organization founded by Christ with its hierarchical structure of offices, with the powers pertaining to these offices, with the many men who, under particular conditions, gain membership in this social organization. All this, indeed, exists and is of the greatest importance for salvation. This society, like any other, has a permanent legal existence which is not discontinued even if we suppose that this Church at a particular time is not operative in any of her powers or in any of her members. A legally founded society has a type of existence different from that of substances. Nevertheless it cannot be denied that, when the Church acts, that is, teaches, confesses the faith, prays, celebrates the Sacrifice of Christ, etc., she reaches a higher degree of actuality than she does by her mere continuing existence. She is a visible society; as really visible she must continually realize her historical, spatio-temporal tangibility through the actions of men. She must become "event" over and over again.

It is not as if these "events" in their separated individuality in space and time founded the Church anew. An actualism of this sort, which would basically deny the social constitution of the Church, tradition, apostolic succession and any real church law of divine right, is foreign to Catholic ecclesiology. But the static and historical continuity of a permanently existing Church does not imply that this Church need not become "event" again and again at definite spatio-temporal points, that she need not pass from a certain potentiality to a particular actuality, and that the whole enduring essence of the Church is not ordered towards this event. If we distinguish in this way between the Church as a mere institution with an enduring social constitution on the one hand, and the Church as "event" on the other, then it follows that she becomes an actual "event", with a spatio-temporal tangibility, in the highest degree when she becomes "event" as the communion of saints, as a society. Naturally she is also present when an individual acts in the Church and for the Church by virtue of the authority of Christ and of an office in the Church. But it cannot be denied that where the Church appears as a communion, *i. e.,* as a plurality of men bound together by a visible occurrence and united by grace, she attains a higher degree of actuality as the Church, than she does when the individual holder of an office brings the Church to actuality by an action of his own in which the other members of the Church take no active part.

Now we ask where and when does the Church become, in the sense indicated above, an "event" in the most intense and actual way? Essentially the Church is the historically continuing presence in the world of the incarnate Word of God. She is the historical tangibility of the salvific will of God as revealed in Christ. Therefore the Church is most tangibly and intensively an "event" where (through the words of consecration) Christ himself is present in his own congregation as the crucified and resurrected Saviour, the fount of salvation; where the Redemption makes itself felt in the congregation by becoming sacramentally visible; where the "New and Eternal Testament" which he founded on the cross is most palpably and actually present in the holy remembrance of its first institution. Therefore the celebration of the Eucharist is the most intensive event of the Church. For by this celebration Christ is not only present in the Church's liturgical solemnity as the Redeemer of

25

his body, as the salvation and lord of the Church; but in the Eucharist the union of the faithful with Christ and with one another is also most tangibly visible, and at the Holy Table is most interiorly realized. Inasmuch as the celebration of the Eucharist is the sacramental anticipation of the heavenly marriage banquet, the final, eternal form of the community of saints shines forth even now in this solemnity just as the source of the Church, Christ's sacrifice on the cross, is present in it.

An essential characteristic of the Eucharistic celebration as a sacramental rite is that it must be localized. (The same holds true for the other sacraments, which are all essentially bound up with the corporeal). It can only be celebrated by one congregation gathered together in one place. But this means that the Church, without prejudice to her social constitution, permanency, universality and relation to all men, is by her inmost nature oriented towards a local concretization and actualization. Therefore the Eucharist as an event in a place not only occurs in the Church; the Church herself becomes in the fullest sense an event only in the local celebration of the Eucharist. That is the fundamental reason why Scripture calls the individual communities *ecclesia,* the same name that the unity of the faithful all over the world possesses. It is not only true that the Eucharist exists because the Church exists; it is also true, if rightly understood, that the Church exists because the Eucharist exists. The Church is and remains, even as a whole, only because she is actualized again and again in the one all-embracing "event" of herself, that is, in the Eucharist. Because this event is essentially localized at one point of time and space and in one local community, therefore the local Church is not only an agency of the universal Church, subsequently founded, and which she could easily dispense with, but is the "event" itself of this universal Church.

If, by some historical catastrophe, a great nation were reduced to a village, then one could no longer correctly say that the nation still existed, that its nature as an historical entity was still realized. But if, *per impossibile,* the Church were reduced to one diocese with its bishop, its legitimate pastor would also be the pope of Rome, and – this is a decisive point – exactly as much would occur in it, as can occur in the universal Church and is the actualization of her nature.[12] She is the proclamation of the dominion of God revealed in the crucified and resurrected flesh of the Son of God as the tribunal of grace over the sins of the world. This proclamation takes place through the legitimate eucharistic celebration of the holy community subjecting itself to the redeeming dominion of God in the remembrance of the Lord's death.

Therefore a local Church is not brought about by an atomizing division of the world-territory of the universal Church, but by the concentration of the Church into her own nature as "event". For this reason, no doubt, the earliest local Church was a bishop's Church. And we might note that the presbyteroi (priests and pastors) originally were not those who were needed

---

[12] Properly to evaluate such an "actualistic" definition of the Church the following must be taken into consideration: a natural society can do or neglect to do many things and still exist; it can neglect to do many things (even though wrongly) that it ought to do; and there are not many things the neglect of which would destroy its existence. In the Church however, there are certain acts which were made a part of her very essence by her divine Founder and which he guaranteed would always take place. Hence the act here lies really in the potency and is not a mere accident of the Church.

27

because there were a number of local communities, but were from the first the senate of the local bishop. As a result the original (episcopal) local communities contained only elements of divine foundation: the holy cultic community of Christ with an apostle or his successor at its head.

What conclusions can be drawn from the relations we have briefly sketched between the universal Church and the local Church (or better, between the Church as she is everywhere and the same Church as she appears in one particular place), which can be applied to the relation between the primacy and the episcopate?

Since the Church is and is intended to be a world Church, insofar as there should be everywhere true adorers of the Father in the Spirit and in the name of Christ, and insofar as this Church, according to her historically perceptible constitution is intended to be one, to that extent the primacy exists. Inasmuch as the same one and universal Church is intended to appear in particular places and precisely in this way to achieve its full consummation, namely, in the celebration of the Eucharist and the rest of the sacraments, to this extent the episcopate exists of divine right.[13] This episcopacy must therefore have all the rights and powers that should belong to it if, on the one hand, the Church as a whole (which does not mean wholly) and in her highest act is to make an historical, tangible appearance

[13] Naturally this does not mean that we could of ourselves, and independent of positive revelation, deduce primacy and episcopate from this principle. But if we already know from positive sources about the positive institution of primacy and episcopate, then we can clearly see their essential connection with this fundamental concept of the Church. For even a positive free institution can conform to the fundamental nature of a thing and does not mean positivistic arbitrariness.

wherever an individual bishop rules; and if, on the other hand, this Church, though "appearing" locally, is the same one which is spread over the whole world and is represented in its catholicity by the pope. We can say that, in the sense and to the extent that the whole Church is completely present in the local Church, the Church's powers of jurisdiction and order are completely present in the local bishop. The papal authority is not more comprehensive in this respect, but in the sense that the pope alone, by divine right of course, represents the unity of the whole Church as the totality of the local Churches. This is quite simply demonstrated by the fact that the pope has no power of order beyond that of the ordinary bishop, although, from an absolute and comprehensive point of view, the *potestas ordinis* is a higher one than the power of jurisdiction.

It will not do merely to accept this equality as the result of an arbitrary divine decree; rather we may and must seek its essential basis, even though we may hold that this can be known only as a result of the express revelation of the fact. Since therefore the Church must make its appearance in particular places, "the episcopate exists in virtue of the same divine institution on which the papacy rests; it too has its rights and duties, which the pope has neither the right nor the power to change. It is therefore a complete misunderstanding ... to suppose ... that the bishops are only instruments of the pope, officials of his without personal responsibility." "According to the constant teaching of the Catholic Church, as expressly declared also by the Vatican Council, the bishops are not mere instruments of the pope, not papal officials without responsibility of their own, but, established by the Holy Spirit and taking the place of the apostles, as true shepherds they feed and rule the flocks entrusted to them. . ."[14] Insofar as the local bishop by his own teaching represents the teaching of the universal Church (which always involves the supreme magisterium of the pope and belief in the unity of the Church), he does not merely relay the teaching of the universal Church or of the pope as if he were a loudspeaker, as though his listeners had to direct their attention past the bishop to what was being said elsewhere in the same connection. On the contrary, in the bishop the Church herself continues her authoritative witness to revealed truth.[15] The case of the powers of order and jurisdiction is similar.

4. The Episcopate and Charismata[16]

The sense of this expression (and by the same token the limits of the concept of the Church's "monarchical" constitution) will perhaps become clearer if we consider the following. In

[14] Therefore "the pope cannot be described as an absolute monarch, even with regard to Church affairs". From a collective Statement of the German bishops in 1875 which was expressly and solemnly approved by Pius IX. Cited with a German translation of this approbation in J. Neuner-H. Roos, *Der Glaube der Kirche in den Urkunden der Lehrverkündigung* (Regensburg, ⁵1958), n. 388a. The complete text in *Katholik,* N. F. Bd. 33 (1875) pp. 209–213.

[15] Cf. D. Palmieri, *Tractatus de Romano Pontifice*² (Prati, 1891), pp. 666 ff. The bishops are *"magistri authentici verique judices, etsi non supremi, in causis fidei et cum singuli in suis sedibus docent, praesumendum est juridice, doctrinam eorum esse catholicam . . ."* For example, when a bishop proscribes the teaching of a particular book (CJC, can. 1395 n. 1), he thereby performs an act of the magisterium which by the nature of the case is not just a repetition of what has always and everywhere been said.

[16] This section will be discussed in a broader context and in more detail to our purpose in Part Three of this book.

the decision of any civil servant it is but the initiative of his superior that is expressed. He may and should indeed show some initiative in preparing this decision, but the content of it is wholly derived from the authority and resolve of his superior, so that whatever occurs in his decision was already "present" in his superior. Now a bishop's decisions are not of this kind. We have already pointed out elsewhere[17] that there is a "charismatic" structure in the Church besides the hierarchical, that is, that in the constitution of the Church the Spirit as Lord of the Church reserves to himself the power and the right to impart impulses to the Church without always and everywhere directing them through the official hierarchical organs of the Church. The same thing can expressly be said about the relation between the hierarchical organs themselves, that is, between the papacy and the bishops. Because the bishops embody the universal Church "on the spot", and insofar as they do so, being the direct representatives of Christ himself and not simply of the pope, they are indeed always dependent on, and responsible to, that unity of the Church in her diffusion which is embodied by the pope, and hence are subject to him; they must preserve "peace and communion" with the Apostolic See. But it does not follow that they are executors of the papal will alone. For they are also hierarchical channels for the impulses of the Holy Spirit, who in the first place accomplishes through them what he wishes done at this particular place in the Church, and furthermore possibly some new insight, a new vitality, new modes of Christian life, private or public, that he wishes to impart via this point to the Church as a whole.

[17] *Das Dynamische in der Kirche* (Freiburg, ²1958), Engl. transl. in preparation.

In his initiative, subject to the immediate guidance of the Spirit of God, the individual bishop must always assure himself of permanent unity and of the assent, at least tacitly given, of the universal Church and the pope. But he is not simply carrying out impulses which emanate from the highest echelon of the Church. Just as he is of divine right, to the extent that he shares in the divine right of the episcopate (even though he as an individual is appointed by the pope), so he is an official organ of such immediate guidance by the Holy Spirit. The approbation of the pope, and thus of the whole Church, is a criterion of his being and remaining a docile organ of this immediate guidance by the Holy Spirit. But this does not mean that his initiative is confined to carrying out an impulse received from the supreme human government of the Church. The pope must also exercise a continuous, official and normal authority over the individual bishop, since the bishop's Church is also a member and a part – though more than this – of the universal Church. To this extent the individual bishop is *also* an executive organ of the papal power. But since his bishop's Church is *the* Church, in that mysterious presence of the whole in the part, which is found only in the Church, impulses from above can directly manifest Christian and ecclesiastical life in him, and through him and his Church to the whole Church. These may be impulses which have not been transmitted through official channels from the higher reaches of the hierarchy.

In the openness to such impulses, to which the bishop (as opposed to the charismatic layman) is obliged by reason of his office, there is a dignity and an obligation which make him even "subjectively" more than a mere official of the pope. This immediate contact of the episcopate with God and his government, in the midst of its "ordinary" dependence on the papacy, may seem complicated, may elude a neat juridical formulation and a clear-cut demarcation of the respective powers of pope and bishop. But this very complexity, these imponderables in the delimitation of the two powers, are grounded in the unique essence of the Church. The Church's own nature shows that the problem of the inalienable powers of the bishops cannot possibly be solved by singling out certain powers and privileges of the bishops over which the pope has no control, as every sort of Gallicanism and Febronianism has always tried to do. The bishop has his most fundamental powers because *the* Church in its actuality appears in him and in his Church; and these same powers of *the* Church are fully vested in the person of the pope for the whole Church.

But the very fact that powers and privileges cannot be divided up between pope and bishop (in the sense of the pope's influence on the bishop having a legally determinable limit) does not mean that the bishop is only an executive official of the pope; and this for the very same reason that the bishop is subject to the pope. Ultimately he is subject to him not because the bishopric represents a small administrative sector of the universal Church, which the bishop administers merely in the name of the universal Church, but because the universal Church is manifest in his diocese. This makes him at once subordinate and independent. Therefore the bishop, too, has a responsibility for the whole Church. Not in the sense that he directly governs her, something which is reserved to the pope alone, but in the sense that he remains at the disposal of the universal Church and of God in such a way that whatever happens in his diocese happens in "communion" with the universal Church, and at the same time happens in such a way that it can be a point of departure from which God's impulse can spread into the universal Church.

As a matter of fact, this has always been so in the history of the Church. If an Athanasius, an Ambrose, an Augustine, a Ketteler (as the pioneer of the Church's modern social teaching), a Cardinal Suhard and many others were not only good bishops of their own dioceses, but signified something irreplaceable for the whole Church, then this greater significance was not theirs as merely private persons (as great theologians, for example) but was essentially based on their quality as bishops. They could never have done what they did, if they had not been bishops; and what they did it was for them to do because they were bishops. The charismatic function of the individual bishops for the universal Church does not detract from the dignity and importance of the papacy. For there have also been many popes in whom office and charismatic mission were united to the blessing of the Church. Only a dictator, not a pope, could see in the free charismata in the Church, in the breathing of the Holy Spirit where it will anything to depreciate, to question or to threaten his permanent office. This is especially true where a charismatic bishop feeds his flock in the name of Christ under the direction of the Holy Spirit. Finally, the popes have constantly emphasized that the *solidus vigor* of the bishops is their honour.[18] This is especially true of that power and vitality which God's Spirit himself grants to the bishops.

Since the pope has the fulness of power, and since any particular jurisdictional power of an individual bishop can, in a given case, be withdrawn by the pope for good cause (or its

[18] Dz. 1828, where the Vatican Council quotes Gregory the Great.

exercise forbidden) – even though the episcopate as such must, as divinely instituted, remain intact – the respective spheres of papal and episcopal authority cannot be sharply delimited, and this very fact makes possible a *human* canon law, its development and modification in accordance with developments in the actual distribution of duties and ordinary powers between the two authorities; whilst the "right" delimitation of these powers (through positive human canon law), that is, appropriate to the matter, to the times and to the intellectual climate, is a process not always to be regulated by fixed constitutional norms. Therefore there is no *legal* tribunal which can ensure that the actual relation between primacy and episcopate, in the canonical delimitation of their respective competences, is proper and objective. Only the influence of the Holy Spirit can continuously assure that the practical balance in positive canon law and in the concrete administration of this law is effected in the manner most beneficial to the Church. If we consider the relation between the two powers from a purely *legal* point of view, then, there is no provision which would effectually prevent the pope so concentrating all power in himself as to leave an episcopate of divine right in name only. For, according to what has been said above, we cannot single out any one power which the pope cannot or may not assume for himself; there is no tribunal on earth which as the pope's superior could declare such action illicit, for the decisions of the Apostolic See are irreformable by any authority. The pope's is the supreme and final jurisdiction, and there is not and cannot be (because of the promised assistance of the Spirit) any ultimate right of resistance, which in practice would dissolve the Church. The continual assistance of the Spirit is the only, the final and decisive guarantee for the

Catholic, that on the whole the properly balanced relationship of a practical kind subsists between the two powers, that according to the exigencies of each successive age neither exaggerated centralization nor episcopalist disintegration, will prevail over the unity of the Church.

Since the solemn definition of the papal primacy there remains practically only one danger, which is the danger of over-centralization in the Church. It was given legal footing and opportunity by the Vatican Council while the decentralizing tendencies operate only through facts and habits.

Hence the ultimate bulwark against this danger can be found only in confidence in the assistance of the Spirit of the Church, which is not legally guaranteed. The Spirit of God is the final guarantee that the episcopate shall retain that scope which, by divine right, it must enjoy. But that is true everywhere: freedom is only where the Spirit is. The field of his free action can indeed be translated into legal norms, but in the last analysis he himself must protect these norms. This shows why the Church cannot have an adequate constitution. Part of herself is the Spirit who alone can guarantee the unity of the Church by the existence of two powers, one of which cannot be adequately reduced to the other in such a way that the Church could really be called a kind of absolute monarchy.

II

PRIMACY, EPISCOPATE, AND APOSTOLIC SUCCESSION

JOSEF RATZINGER

THERE is a paradox in the term Roman Catholic, whereby religious statistics today distinguish the community of the faithful in communion with the bishop of Rome from other "Catholicisms". And this verbal paradox expresses a significant theological problem. "Catholic", like "ecumenical", signifies the transcending of all spatial limits, the claim to embrace the whole world. When *catholicus* became the *cognomen* of *Christianus,* this universality was intended to do away with territorially restricted sects and so, as it were, bring about religious-statistical uniformity.[1] Now when "Roman" is added to "Catholic", this reflects not only the scandalous split within the *Catholica* itself, which is the principal reason why such a title became necessary, but also it would seem to imply a tacit withdrawal of the former title, spatial universality now being particularized and narrowed down to an individual place.

---

[1] Pacian of Barcelona, *Ep.* 1, 4, in C. Kirch, *Enchiridion Fontium Historiae Ecclesiasticae Antiquae* (1941), p. 627: *"Christianus mihi nomen est, catholicus cognomen."* Catholicity as a concrete sign of the true Church is especially clear in Augustine. Cf. F. Hofmann, *Der Kirchenbegriff des hl. Augustinus* (Munich, 1933); J. Ratzinger, *Volk und Haus Gottes in Augustins Lehre von der Kirche* (Munich, 1954).

In the unique polarity relating these two words we capture in arresting fashion the interrelation between unity and fulness, between primacy and episcopate. While the name "Roman Catholic" points to the phenomenon of the split in Catholicism, it reveals at a deeper level the basis of this split by bringing to light that fundamental conception of unity and catholicity which has always divided the minds of men and continues to do so.

The plan of John XXIII for the council has once more brought this problem into the centre of theological inquiry, and, after decades of concentration on "Roman", which followed the Vatican Council, has again directed more attention to the other side of the scale, to "Catholic", with which, to be sure, "Roman" forms a paradoxical unity, so that one separated from the other would no longer be itself. Theologians are preparing to rewrite the textbook tracts "De episcopo" and "De conciliis" now that they have been able to bring such a high degree of clarity to the tract "De primatu"[2]. We here attempt a modest contribution to this discussion by a study of the idea of succession. It is, however, important to avoid false problems and making

---

[2] Recent attempts to develop the traditional teaching *De episcopo* are K. Rahner, *Episcopate and Primacy,* Part I of this book; H. Schauf, *De Corpore Christi Mystico* (Freiburg, 1959), pp. 305–310; 298–301 (a reproduction of the theses of C. Schrader); K. Hofstetter, "Der römische Primatsanspruch im Lichte der Heilsgeschichte", *Una Sancta* 11 (1956), pp. 176–183; O. Karrer, „Das kirchliche Amt in katholischer Sicht", *Una Sancta* 14 (1959), pp. 39–48; F. Amiot and J. Colson, "Évêque", *Catholicisme* IV, pp. 781–820; J. Gewiess, M. Schmaus and K. Mörsdorf, „Bischof", *Lexikon für Theologie und Kirche* II[2], col. 491–505, with a full bibliography. Cf. also the survey article "Was ist ein Bischof", *Herder-Korrespondenz* 12 (1957/1958), pp. 188–194.

irrelevant matters or others in no need of clarification the object of misapplied subtlety. We must rather concentrate on those truly open questions the discussion of which will afford some hope of more than verbal progress in the quest to understand the Church's nature, and thus can render a genuine service to divided Christianity.

1. The Teaching of the Church on Primacy and Episcopate

Let us then first ask what is the certain teaching of the Church, the data which we can and must presuppose in discussion both among Catholics and with others. First, it is the certain teaching of the Church that the pope has immediate, ordinary, truly episcopal power of jurisdiction over the whole Church.[3] The Vatican Council calls the primacy of the pope the apostolic primacy, and the Roman See the apostolic see.[4] Thus in the realm of doctrine the pope, in his official capacity, is infallible, his *ex cathedra* decisions being irreformable *ex sese*[5] and not in virtue of the Church's subsequent confirmation. So far as *communio* is concerned, the other pillar of the Church, it follows that only he who is in communion with the pope lives in the true *communio* of the body of the Lord, *i.e.*, in the true Church.[6]

Contrasted with these certain truths about the pope stand a

---

[3] Dz. 1827, 1831.

[4] Dz. 1832, 1836.

[5] Dz. 1839.

[6] The two orders of *"communio"* and *"doctrine"* are expressly placed side by side in Dz. 1827: *". . . ita ut, custodita cum Romano Pontifice tam communionis quam ejusdem fidei professionis unitate, Ecclesia Christi sit unus grex sub uno summo pastore."*

series of truths, equally certain, about the nature of the episcopal office. If on the one hand the papal see is called the apostolic see and his primacy is called apostolic, it is also true that the bishops *"in Apostolorum locum successerunt"*.[7] While the pope is accorded ordinary episcopal power in the whole Church, so that one might have the impression that the bishops were only executive organs of this power, it is declared on the other hand that they are "instituted by the Holy Ghost"[8] and that they are "of divine right".[9] That is, they are not of papal right; the pope cannot suppress them since they are as much part and parcel of the divinely appointed structure of the Church as he.

Dom Olivier Rousseau recently drew the attention of theologians to a sadly neglected document, which he rightly judges to be an authentic commentary on the Vatican Council. One could indeed look on it as a sort of postscript to the tract *De episcopo* which the Council did not embark upon. It is, at any rate, a most important supplement for it provides the key to the full meaning of the Vatican decrees. It is the "Collective Statement of the German Episcopate concerning the Circular of the German Imperial Chancellor in respect of the Coming Papal Election", of the year 1875, which received the express and unqualified endorsement of Pius IX.[10] Rousseau summarizes the content of this document in seven points.

---

[7] Dz. 1828.
[8] Dz. 1828.
[9] CJC, can. 329, par. 1.
[10] O. Rousseau, "La vraie Valeur de l'Épiscopat dans l'Église d'après d'importants documents de 1875", *Irénikon* 29 (1956), pp. 121–150. Rousseau rightly pointed out that this is a text that ought to be included in "Denzinger".

1. "The pope cannot arrogate to himself the
   episcopal rights, nor substitute his
   power for that of the bishops;
2. the episcopal jurisdiction has not been
   absorbed in the papal jurisdiction;
3. the pope was not given the entire fulness
   of the bishops' powers by the decrees of
   the Vatican Council;
4. he has not virtually taken the place of
   each individual bishop;
5. he cannot put himself in the place of a
   bishop in each single instance, *vis-à-vis*
   governments;
6. the bishops have not become instruments of
   the pope;
7. they are not officials of a foreign sovereign
   in their relations with their own governments."[11]

If, in the light of this document, one re-examines the Vatican
pronouncements on the primacy, then it cannot be denied that
they are much deeper and also much less simple than theological
textbooks commonly indicate. Basically they are shot through
with the same dialectic which characterizes all the pronouncements of this Council, the language of which, often oversimplied,
is yet in fact remarkably nuanced. H. U. von Balthasar has

---

[11] The German translation from Rousseau in *Una Sancta* 12 (1957), p. 227.
(The English was checked with the original French of Rousseau.) In
Rousseau's article, footnote 6, a similar statement by Cardinal van Roey
is mentioned. Note 4 refers to a corresponding declaration of the English
bishops and of Cardinal Dechamps. The texts of the double acknowledge-
ment of the Pope are on p. 225 ff.

demonstrated the dialectical character of the first part of the Vatican decrees by pointing out that the Council did not simply define the existence of a natural knowledge of God; rather its pronouncements on this issue are pervaded with a sublime dialectic, inasmuch as the *certo cognosci posse* in one section is balanced in the other by emphasis of a lack of that *firma certitudo,* that might be attainable, easily and free from error, by all mankind. We thus get the following scheme:

Humana ratio per se   in presenti generis humani conditione

certo cognoscere potest   firmam *certitudinem* revelatio
tribuit *omnibus* hominibus
expedite et nullo admixto errore.[12]

The *certo* thus appears at once under the sign of *sic* and *non*. The Council provides no simple formula such as the theologian is always (and rightly) seeking. Rather, it obviously believes that it can express the full content only in the paradoxical tension of *sic et non*. This same dialectic is also visible in the next paragraph, concerning the discernibility of revelation through miracles. Here the *certo* is capped with a *certissime,* and becomes a more acute problem because the subject of this firm certainty is not the abstract *humana ratio per se,* but the real reason of the average man. Yet this strengthened *sic* is contrasted with a strengthened *non,* for it is also stressed that this perception is "free obedience", which a man can resist or escape.[13] Here, too,

[12] Dz. 1785 ff. Cf. H. U. von Balthasar, *Karl Barth* (Cologne, 1951), p. 318; and in general, pp. 314–335.
[13] Dz. 1790: ". . . *signa sunt certissima et omnium intelligentiae accommodata.*" The "*resistere posse*" in Dz. 1791.

the Council remains committed to the whole of reality, which can only be expressed by the dialectic interplay of two series of statements, each of which is of itself inadequate.

Now if we consider the paragraph *De R. Pontificis et episcoporum jurisdictione*,[13a] often lightly passed over, then we see that it brings into the doctrine on the primacy that same dialectic which characterizes the Council's notion of faith and revelation. Once again there are two series of statements confronting each other and not easily brought into a simple unity. Only as they stand can they approximately express the whole, no less complicated, reality. To borrow the expression of Heribert Schauf, the Church is not like a circle, with a single centre, but like an ellipse with two foci, primacy and episcopate.[14]

We can express this in terms of the history of dogma. In the centuries-long struggle between episcopalism–conciliarism on the one side and papalism on the other, the Vatican Council is not at all a clear victory for the latter, as it might well seem to the superficial observer. According to the classical papalism of the Middle Ages, "the hierarchical culmination of the priesthood in the episcopate, *i.e.*, the jurisdictional superiority of the bishop" was "a disciplinary measure of the Church", explained by the consideration that "the pope, simply as a matter of fact, is not in a position to shepherd and govern all the faithful". The pope can, according to this theory, "define, narrow or even suppress the jurisdictional power of a bishop at any time".[15] The Vatican

---

[13a] Dz. 1828.   [14] H. Schauf, p. 307, *op. cit.* in footnote 2.

[15] This was the view of one of the earliest advocates of papalism, Herveus Natalis (d. 1323). The quotations are from L. Hoedl, *De Jurisdictione. Ein unveröffentlichter Traktat des Herveus Natalis O. P. über die Kirchengewalt* (Munich, 1959), p. 11 (Mitteilungen des Grabmann-Instituts, edited by M.

Council stands for a condemnation of papalism as much as of episcopalism. Actually, it brands both doctrines as erroneous and, in place of one-sided solutions stemming from late theology or power politics, it establishes the dialectic of the reality we have from Christ. Precisely in disclaiming any simple formula which would satisfy reason, it attests its respect for truth.

The fact that, according to the Vatican Council, not only episcopalism but also papalism in the narrower sense must be regarded as a condemned doctrine, must be impressed much more efficaciously on the Christian consciousness than has been done to date. In the great historical struggle between the two powerful movements, the Vatican Council takes neither side, but creates a new position, which, transcending all human constitutional thought, formulates the special quality of the Church, which comes, not from the discretion of men, but in the final analysis, from the word of God.

Our investigation into the certain teaching of the Church has thus led us into the midst of the problems connected with these matters of certainty, and, of course, also made clear their limits. Episcopate and primacy in the Church are, according to the Catholic Faith, of divine origin. There can be no question, consequently, of the Catholic theologian playing one off against the other; he can only attempt to understand more deeply the vital relationship between the two. Thus he will help, by his

Schmaus, Heft 2). For the history of the origins of papalism: J. Ratzinger, "Der Einfluß des Bettelordensstreites auf die Entwicklung der Lehre vom päpstlichen Universalprimat", *Theologie in Geschichte und Gegenwart* (Schmaus-Festschrift) edited by J. Auer and H. Volk (Munich, 1957), pp. 697–724; for further history of the problem: F. Cayré, *Patrologie et histoire de la théologie II* (Paris, 1955) pp. 620ff.; 681–696.

study, towards the proper development of this relationship, which, of course, is realized through men and is the mould, ever open to human violation, of the divine data and commands.

Father Karl Rahner has tried to explain this relationship more exactly in the light of the notion of *communio*.[16] This remains undoubtedly the central point of attack since the Church by her inmost nature is *communio*, fellowship with and in the body of the Lord.[17] Father Rahner's reflection leads to the corrollary, that the Church of the Incarnate Word is in turn the Church of the "word" and not merely the Church of the sacraments. Sacrament *and* word are the two pillars on which the Church stands.[18] Once again, in the relation between these two, we find an irreducible polarity of unity and duality, such as is the sign of living being, that precedes the constructions of logic and can never be entirely circumscribed by them.

If now in our quest we begin with the notion of word, we are led to the notion of *successio*. This notion was not derived

[16] Cf. Part One of this book. H. Schauf, *op. cit.*, critical of Rahner, suggests a solution based on the biblical idea of multiple witness and is thus closer to a theology of the "word" and an interpretation which I also favour. Yet I would like to point out, against Schauf, that besides his notion, and indeed prior to it, the development of the question from the notion of *communio* is possible and justified. The question has two aspects, which, in accordance with the dual structure of the Church arising from sacrament and word, do not exclude but complete each other.

[17] M.-J. Le Guillou, O. P., "Église et communion. Essai d'ecclésiologie comparée." *Istina* 7 (1959), pp. 33–82 with full bibliography. An historical treatment in W. Elert, *Abendmahl und Kirchengemeinschaft in der alten Kirche hauptsächlich des Ostens* (Berlin, 1954); J. Ratzinger, *Volk und Haus Gottes in Augustins Lehre von der Kirche* (Munich, 1954).

[18] Cf. the passage from the Vatican Council quoted in note 6: Dz. 1827.

45

(at least not primarily) from a consideration of *communio,* but rather from the struggle for the "word", and is more germane to this context, even though objectively it necessarily connotes the aspect of *communio.* The problem of primacy and episcopate is mirrored in the notion of succession inasmuch as it is said on the one hand that the bishops are the successors of the apostles, while on the other, the predicate *apostolicus* is reserved to the pope in a special way. Thus the question arises whether there is a double succession and therefore a double participation in apostolicity. It would seem better first to inquire into the nature of succession itself, and then to weigh the meaning of the word *apostolicus* in connection with the notion of succession.

2. Reflections on the Nature of the Apostolic Succession in General

The notion of succession, as the German Protestant theologian von Campenhausen has shown, was clearly formulated in the anti-gnostic polemics of the second century.[19] Its purpose was to oppose to the pseudo-apostolic tradition of Gnosis, the true apostolic tradition of the Church. Thus from the beginning it was very closely connected with the question of true apostolicity. But first and foremost, it is clear that *successio* and *traditio,* as first used, meant practically the same thing, and indeed were expressed by the same word διαδοχή, which meant both tradition and succession.[20] "Tradition" is never a simple, anonymous

[19] Hans von Campenhausen, *Kirchliches Amt und geistliche Vollmacht in den ersten drei Jahrhunderten* (Tübingen, 1953), pp. 163–194.
[20] Cf. E. Caspar, "Die älteste römische Bischofsliste", *Schriften der Königsberger gelehrten Gesellschaft,* Geisteswiss. Klasse 2, 4 (1926); Th.

passing on of doctrine, but is personal, is the living word, concretely realized in the faith. And "succession" is not a taking over of official powers, which then are at the disposal of their possessor, but is rather a dedication to the word, an office of bearing witness to the treasure with which one has been entrusted. The office is superior to its holder, so that he is entirely overshadowed by that which he has received; he is, as it were – to adopt the image of Isaias and John the Baptist – only a voice which renders the word articulate in the world.

The office, the apostolic succession is grounded in the word. That is as true today as then. What was the situation then? To the Christianity of the Church the Gnostics opposed their own tangled philosophy of religion, which they represented as a secret tradition from the apostles. Against this the defenders of the Church declared that it was in the Church that those communites were to be found in which the apostles themselves had laboured, or which had received apostolic letters. In these communities the line of succession could be traced back, as it were, to the lips of an apostle. The men who were now their leaders could trace their spiritual lineage back to the apostles. Now if there can exist anywhere a knowledge of the oral heritage of the apostles, it must exist in these communities and they are the true measure of that which alone may rightly be called "apostolic".

We see here very clearly how in fact succession equals tradition.

Klauser, "Die Anfänge der römischen Bischofsliste", *Bonner Zeitschrift für Theologie und Seelsorge* 8 (1931), pp. 193–213, esp. 196. A systematic treatment of the connection between tradition and succession: G. Söhngen, "Überlieferung und apostolische Verkündigung", *Die Einheit in der Theologie* (Munich, 1952), pp. 305–323.

Succession means cleaving to the apostolic word, just as tradition means the continuance of authorized witnesses. Beyond the instrumental rôle of Gnosis, as Dr. von Campenhausen has shown, the Church, in formulating the principle of succession (tradition), adapted for herself a method of the ancient philosophers who, in their schools, had first practised a way of drawing up lists of succession.[21] This may be so, though the state of the sources hardly allows a fully definitive judgment. For the rest, must not the word of God and the reality based on it always make use of human relationships in order to express itself among men? However, if by this von Campenhausen meant to show that biblical theology takes precedence over a later, and thus secondary, theology of succession-tradition,[22]

---

[21] H. von Campenhausen, *op. cit.,* p. 183. L. Köp emphasizes Jewish precedents in the article *"Bischofsliste"*, RAC II, pp. 407–415, esp. 407ff. For the further development of the idea in Roman juridical thought, cf. G. Tellenbach, "Auctoritas A'', RAC I, pp. 904–909: p. 906: "The jurist Tertullian introduced into Christian teaching the conception of Roman private law, according to which each legal predecessor was for the possessor of a thing the *auctor,* that is, the guarantor and witness. The apostles, as the first recipients of the teaching . . ., passed it on to the communities or their leaders and these in turn to their successors. Thus the apostles and the earlier bishops are the *auctores* of the later ones: the legitimate line of succession guarantees the faith and the continuance of apostolic *auctoritas.* Tradition and authority enter into a firm relationship to each other. . ." Tellenbach also cites U. Gmelin, *Römische Herrscheridee und päpstliche Autorität* (1937).

[22] This is suggested on p. 176ff. It is maintained (on p. 177) that even Irenaeus was much more of a biblical theologian than is usually recognized and admitted. This is, of course, true in the sense that Irenaeus uses Scripture to a great extent and that his whole mentality is nourished by it. But the use of Scripture and the biblical principle are nevertheless two different things.

then we must regard this as an error. Christians had already formulated the principle of *successio-traditio* before they yet understood the New Testament as "Scripture". Therefore they could not formulate this as a biblical principle from the New Testament. Moreover, because of the influence of Marcion, the notion of "Scripture" was influenced by Gnosis to an even greater extent than that of tradition.[23]

Let us not be deceived: The existence of writings which concerned the New Covenant and were acknowledged as apostolic, does not yet imply the existence of a New Testament as "Scripture". From writings to Scripture there is a long way to go. It is well known, and should not be overlooked, that the New Testament nowhere shows the consciousness of being Scripture. To it, the Old Testament is Scripture while the gospel of Christ is precisely "Spirit", which teaches understanding of the Scripture.[24] The notion of the New Testament as Scripture is at this early date completely unimaginable, even after "office" has already clearly emerged as the form of παράδοσις. This open situation whereby acknowledged New Testament writings are extant without there being any New Testament principle of Scripture or a clear concept of what is canonical lasted until well into the second century, right into the period of conflict with Gnosticism. Before the idea of New Testament Scripture, as a "canon", was formulated the Church had already worked out another notion of canon. She had her Scripture indeed in the

[23] Cf. A. von Harnack, *Dogmengeschichte I* (Tübingen, ⁵1931), pp. 372ff.; A. Jülicher and E. Fascher, *Einleitung in das Neue Testament* (Tübingen, ⁷1931), pp. 478ff.

[24] Cf. especially the basic expositions of 2 Cor. 3; on this the important explanations of G. Schrenk in ThWNT I, pp. 766ff.

Old Testament, but this Scripture needed a canon, that is, a rule of interpretation, in accordance with the New Christian Covenant. This the Church found in tradition, guaranteed by succession. "Canon", as von Harnack once drastically formulated it, "was originally the rule of faith; actually, Scripture entered into it only afterwards."[25] Before the New Testament itself became Scripture, it was faith which interpreted the "Scripture," *i.e.,* the Old Testament. Of course the other extreme, also erroneous, must be rejected. The Church opposed Gnosis with the living διαδοχή which is, as we have seen, *traditio* and *successio* all in one: the word bound up with a witness, and the witness bound to the word. But that did not mean that the Church intended to canonize an oral tradition of doctrine as something parallel to Scripture. Quite the contrary: she formulated the principle precisely to defend herself against the gnostic allegation of a παράδοσις ἄγραφος (an unwritten tradition). The uninterrupted διαδοχή (παράδοσις) ἀποστολική of the Church was for the early anti-gnostic theologians precisely the proof that there was no such thing as the παράδοσις ἄγραφος which the Gnostics preached (at least in the form alleged by the Gnostics). Whatever might be the terminological dependence, παράδοσις (διαδοχή) meant something entirely different on the two sides — in fact the exact opposite. In Gnosis it meant exhaustive doctrines of allegedly apostolic origin. But in the theology of the Church it meant the connection of the living faith with the authority of the Church, embodied in the episcopal succession. The Church did not appeal to the παράδοσις in order to assert unwritten apostolic doctrines

[25] A. von Harnack, *op. cit.,* vol. II, p. 87, note 3. Cf. also H. Bacht, "Die Rolle der Tradition in der Kanonbildung", *Catholica* 12 (1958), pp. 16–37.

as a source of revelation parallel to Scripture; but precisely in order to deny the existence of such a secret heritage. For her, παράδοσις meant that in the community of the New Covenant the "Scriptures" (*i.e.*, the Old Testament) are subordinate to the living interpretation of the faith which has come down from the apostles.[25a] The central instruments of this interpretation are the New Testament Scriptures and the Creed which sums them up, but they are instruments in the service of the living faith, which has its concrete form in the διαδοχή.[26]

To put it still another way, there is in the Church, according to the early anti-gnostic theologians, a "tradition" insofar as the primary seat of the *auctoritas apostolica* is the Church preaching the living word, but not in the sense that the Church has preserved secret communications from the time of the apostles. One could also say there is a tradition in the Church, but no traditions. The notion of a tradition is orthodox; that of traditions is gnostic.[27]

Thus it emerges that apostolic tradition and apostolic succession define each other. The succession is the external form of the tradition, and tradition is the content of the succession. At the

---

[25a] This of course by no means excludes the existence of revealed truths officially handed down in the Church, which did not however find their way into the New Testament.

[26] The consequences of this for the systematic theology of today cannot be explored here. Some important suggestions in K. Rahner, *Inspiration in the Bible* (Engl. transl.: New York, 1961), esp. pp. 72–76.

[27] Of course, by this we do not mean that the notion of traditions cannot also appear in a legitimate sense, in accordance with church teaching. We merely affirm that it was first formulated in Gnosticism and accordingly in gnostic fashion. A useful contribution to this subject is J. N. Bakhuizen van den Brink's "Traditio im theologischen Sinn", *Vigiliae christ.* 13 (1959), pp. 65–68.

same time this relationship contains the justification of both principles. In fact, there is really only one principle, the decisive one which separates Catholic Christianity (Roman or Greek) from that group of Christians who renounce the *cognomen* Catholic, and are content with the Gospel alone for their title.[28] For to accord priority to the living word of preaching over Scripture alone is genuinely in keeping with the New Testament; and the Christian theologians who, in debate with the Gnostics, expressed the Church's consciousness of herself in the sense outlined above, depict a community which, in this essential kernel of its self-knowledge, still remains identical with the Church mirrored in the writings of the New Testament. The relevance of this becomes clear when we compare it with the following statement of Oskar Cullman, which can be taken as a classic formulation of Protestant thinking on the notion of succession: "Only one text in the New Testament – the paragraph, already mentioned, of the prayer of the High Priest, Jo. 17, 20 – speaks expressly of the relation of the apostles to the Church which succeeds them. In it, the continuation of the apostles' efficacy is subordinate not to the principle of succession, but to the *word* of the apostles: 'those who believe through their word'."[29]

---

[28] This would be the sort of criterion enabling us to decide whether and to what extent a particular Christian church might be regarded as part of the Catholic formulation of the Christian faith.

Translator's note: The author is here referring to the Lutheran Church in Germany, usually known as "Evangelical".

[29] O. Cullmann, *Peter* (London, 1955), p. 248f. Related to this is what Barth says on the problem of succession: K. Barth, *Kirchliche Dogmatik I* (Zurich, 1947), pp. 97–101. For the standpoint of the United Evangelical-Lutheran Church of Germany, cf. its "Erklärung zur Apostolischen Suk-

But can we really treat succession and the word as opposites? Undoubtedly, only if we take the word to mean exclusively the written word, *i.e.*, a book. But can we really assume that the New Testament is thinking of a book when it speaks of the word? It is true that later generations come to the faith through the word; but in the perspective of the Bible, not as *readers*, but as *hearers* of the word. Who is not reminded, in this context, of the words of Saint Paul: "How then are they to call upon him in whom they do not believe? But how are they to believe him whom they have not heard? And how are they to hear, if no one preaches? And how are men to preach unless they be sent? As it is written, 'How beautiful are the feet of those who preach the gospel of peace; of those who bring glad tidings of good things'."[30]

The word is then, on the view of the New Testament, the word that is *heard,* thus the word that is preached, but not the word that is read.

That is to say that if true apostolic succession is bound up with the word, it cannot be bound up merely with a book, but must, as the succession of the word, be a succession of preachers, which in turn cannot exist without a "mission", *i.e.*, a personal continuity reaching back to the apostles. Precisely for the sake of the word, which in the New Covenant is not to consist in dead letters but in a living voice, a living succession is necessary. Ultimately the theology of word and Scripture in the New Testament supplies even stronger confirmation of the concept of

---

zession", *Informationsdienst der VELKD* 1958, pp. 4–13; P. Brunner, *Vom Amt des Bischofs* (Berlin, 1955) and "Bischof IV", *Lexikon für Theologie und Kirche II*, col. 505 f.

[30] Rom. 10:14 ff.

succession as formulated by early anti-gnostic theology than the increasingly widespread recognition that the rite of conferring an office by imposition of hands, taken over from Judaism, must go back to the Jewish beginnings of Christianity.[31]

Finally, it is precisely and only in such an understanding of the gift of the Word to the Church, that man is forced, continually and in all earnestness, into the position of a "Hearer of the Word", a hearer who himself has not power over the Word, but remains in that purely receptive frame of mind which is called "believing"[32]. Such "believing" is stripped of all individualistic limitation. Because it is based on "hearing", it is continuously directed to a "thou", to that great community of the faithful who are called to become "one person" in Christ.[33]

To sum up, the Church at first opposed to the gnostic notion of secret, unwritten traditions not Scripture but the principle of succession. Apostolic succession is essentially the living presence of the Word in the person of the witness. The unbroken continuity of witnesses follows from the nature of the Word as *auctoritas* and *viva vox*.

---

[31] Cf. E. Lohse, *Die Ordination im Spätjudentum und im Neuen Testament,* (Göttingen, 1951); O. Linton, "Kirche und Amt des NT", *Ein Buch von der Kirche,* edited by Aulen, Fridrichsen *et. al.* (Göttingen, 1951), pp. 110–144; A. Volkmann, "Evangelisch-katholische Gedanken zur Frage der Successio Apostolica", *Una Sancta* 10 (1955), pp. 42–54; W. Richter, "Apostolische Sukzession und die Vereinigte Evangelisch-Lutherische Kirche Deutschlands", *Una Sancta* 14 (1959), pp. 48–54. The last two authors cited, both Evangelical theologians, especially in connection with Lohse, present notions of apostolic succession which tend strongly towards the Catholic. Concerning our remarks against Cullmann, cf. O. Karrer, *Um die Einheit der Christen* (Frankfurt, 1953), pp. 166 ff.
[32] Cf. R. Guardini, "Evangelisches Christentum in katholischer Sicht heute", *Una Sancta* 13 (1958), pp. 225–233.   [33] Gal. 3:8.

3. Papal Succession and Episcopal Succession:
Their Relation and Differences

The anti-gnostic theology of succession extends a good deal further than we have yet shown into the problematic area of the question of "primacy and episcopate". In proof of their error the Gnostics were not referred to the episcopal office as such in the Church, but to the apostolic sees, *i.e.,* those sees where apostles had once worked or which had received apostolic letters. In other words not every episcopal see was apostolic, but only that limited number which stood in a unique and special relationship to the apostles. These were the centres of apostolic witness, with which all other sees had to align themselves. Tertullian, for example, expresses this very clearly when he refers each area to its respective apostolic see with the following words: *"Proxima est tibi Achaia, habes Corinthum. Si non longe es a Macedonia, habes Philippos; si potes in Asiam tendere, habes Ephesum; si autem Italiae adiaces, habes Romam, unde nobis quoque (i.e.,* the Africans) *auctoritas praesto est."*[34]

Then in the following sentence he declares that Rome occupies a particularly prominent position among the apostolic sees, since it can call three apostles its very own, Peter, Paul and John. The same idea lies behind the famous saying of St. Irenaeus concerning the *potentior principalitas* of Rome, with which all other Churches must agree: Irenaeus too envisages the Church as covered with a network of apostolic sees, among which the See of Peter and Paul possesses unequivocal pre-eminence as the criterion of the succession-tradition.[35]

---

[34] *De praescr. haer.* 36, 2 (CChL I 216).
[35] *Adv. haer.* 3, 3, 1 and 2, PG 7, pp. 844ff., esp. p. 848. The same con-

From this we can draw a number of important conclusions:

1. Early Catholic theology in the context of the question of succession, uses the word "apostolic" in a very precise and strictly defined sense. It is used to designate only that very limited number of sees standing in a special, verifiable, historical relation to the apostles, a relation other sees do not enjoy.[36]

2. This is not in any way to dispute the apostolic succession of all bishops. But the majority of bishops, those not in apostolic sees, succeed only by a circuitous route, *i.e.,* through an apostolic see. They are apostolic indirectly, not directly. They are legitimately apostolic only because they are in communion with an apostolic see. The practice of "communion" in the ancient Church, which must be considered the means whereby Church unity was then effected, worked on this principle. The apostolic sees were the criterion

viction is to be seen already in Hegesippus: Eusebius, HE IV 22, 2f. The ancient Church's theology of the apostolic sees was notably clarified by P. Batiffol, esp. *L'Église naissante et le Catholicisme* (Paris, 1909) and *Le Siège apostolique* (Paris, 1924).

[36] This fact seems to me to be conclusive in deciding the controversial question, to whom to ascribe the so-called Edict of Callist, mentioned in the *De Pudicitia.* Dr. Poschmann, above all others, has sought to prove its non-Roman origin. When the author of the edict is addressed as *"apostolice"* in 21, 5 (CChL II 1326) it must be said that this unequivocally refers to Rome. The word *apostolicus* could not be used simply in some arbitrary fashion; it had in relation to a bishop a strictly defined sense which was understood by everyone. It referred to the incumbent of a *sedes apostolica,* that is, in the West, it referred to Rome. It remains true that in this context Tertullian uses the word with biting irony throughout the whole passage. For the rest, H. Bacht, quoting L. M. Dewailly, rightly remarks in the article "Apostolisch, *Lexikon für Theologie und Kirche* I², col II" 758, that the history of the word "apostolic" yet remains to be written.

of the true, *i.e.*, the Catholic communion. Whoever was in communion with them was in the Catholic Church, for these sees could not, by their very nature, exist outside the Church.[37] Thus, the Catholicity of a see was not measured simply by its size, but by its "weight", or importance; that importance, however, depended on apostolicity.

3. To this extent it can be said that this theology draws a real distinction between two forms of apostolic succession, one direct and one indirect. The latter needs communion with the former in order to remain Catholic, and, therefore in the full sense of the word, apostolic.

4. Among the apostolic sees, there is in turn *the* apostolic see, Rome, which bears approximately the same relation to the other apostolic sees as they do to those which are not directly apostolic. Thus Rome is the final, proper, and self-sufficient criterion of Catholicity.[38]

Taken together, these points establish that the theology of apostolic succession, at the moment when it was first formulated as such and when the Church thus first undertook consciously to define her own nature, *i. e.,* to formulate the "canon" of her

---

[37] L. Hertling, "Communio und Primat", *Miscellanea historiae Pontificia* VII (Rome, 1943), pp. 3–48.

[38] Awareness of this is clearly reflected for example: in Tertullian, Adv. Praxean 1, 5 (CChL II 1159): "*Nam idem tunc episcopum Romanum, agnoscentem iam prophetias Montani, Priscae, Maximillae et ex ea agnitione pacem ecclesiis Asiae et Phrygiae inferentem, falsa de ipsis prophetis . . . adseverando et praecessorum eius auctoritates defendendo coegit et litteras pacis revocare iam emissas et a proposito recipiendorum charismatum concessare.*" It has often been remarked that the conduct of Pope Victor in the controversy about the date of Easter can only be explained in terms of such an awareness. Cf. L. Hertling, *op. cit.*; M.-J. Le Guillou, *op. cit.*, esp. p. 39.

being, was neither an episcopal theology nor indeed a papal theology. It was dual, distinguishing the "episcopate" from the apostolic sees – the latter supremely embodied in the one See of Rome. If succession is the concrete external form of the word then from the very beginning it exhibits that most intense (perhaps scandalous) concreteness, which consists in being ultimately bound to the Roman line of succession. Here all anonymity ceases. The concrete name inexorably challenges men to take up a position. This name is the most acute form of that extreme concreteness into which God came when he assumed not merely a human name, but the flesh of man – the flesh of the Church. May it not also arouse the most acute form of that scandal which this "folly" of God provokes?

One further point. It is clear that the duality, set up by the earliest theology of succession with its emphasis on apostolic sees, has nothing to do with the later patriarchal theory. Confusion between the primitive claim of the apostolic see and the administrative claim of the patriarchal city characterizes the tragic beginning of conflict between Constantinople and Rome. The theory of a patriarchal constitution, which especially since the council of Chalcedon, has been held up against the Roman claim and which has tried to force the latter into its own mould, mistakes the whole character of the Roman claim, which is based on an entirely different principle. The patriarchal principle is post-Constantinian, its instinct administrative, its application thus closely tied up with political and geographic data. The Roman claim, by contrast, must be understood in the light of the originally theological notion of the apostolic sees. The more New Rome (which could not dream of calling itself "apostolic") obscured the old idea of the apostolic see in favour of the patriarchal concept, the more Old Rome emphasized the completely different origin and nature of its authority.[39] Indeed, this is something entirely different from a primacy of honour among patriarchs, since it exists on quite another plane, wholly independent of such administrative schemes. The overshadowing of the old theological notion of the apostolic see – an original part, after all, of the Church's understanding of her own nature – by the theory of five patriarchs must be understood as the real harm done in the quarrel between East and West. The mischief has had its effect on the West to the extent that, though the notion of apostolic authority has remained unharmed, nevertheless a far-reaching administrative-patriarchal conception of the importance of the Roman See has necessarily developed, making it no easier for those outside the fold to grasp the real heart of the Roman claim in contrast to other claims.

The actual content of the Roman claim is expressed by the concept of the apostolic see in centripetal fashion, yet the same concept also connotes an orientation to the fulness of the Church. We get, therefore, the following picture: The Church is the living presence of the divine Word. This presence is made concrete in those persons (the bishops) whose basic function is to hold fast to the word, who are, then, the personal embodiment of "tradition" (παράδοσις) and to this extent are in the apostolic line of "succession" (διαδοχή). Conspicuous among the successors of the apostles is the line of the apostolic sees, which ultimately is concentrated in the See of Peter and Paul. This is the touchstone of all apostolic succession. Thus the "bishops" are

[39] Cf. H. Wagenvoort and G. Tellenbach, "Auctoritas", RAC I, pp. 902–909, esp. pp. 908 f.

first of all referred to Rome, for only communion with Rome gives them Catholicity and that fulness of apostolicity without which they would not be true bishops. Without communion with Rome one cannot be in the *Catholica*. This reference of the bishops to Rome is the primary relationship to be ascertained.

On the other hand, the episcopal see of Rome itself does not stand in isolation, devoid of relationships. It creates their Catholicity for other sees, but precisely for this reason it also needs Catholicity. It sets up the essential order of Catholicity; and precisely because of this it needs the reality of Catholicity. Just as, on the one hand, it guarantees essential Catholicity, so on the other hand real Catholicity stands warranty for it. Just as the other sees need the apostolic testimony of Rome in order to be Catholic, so Rome needs their Catholic testimony, the testimony of real fulness, in order to remain true. Without the testimony of reality, Rome would negate its own meaning. A pope who would excommunicate the entire episcopate could never exist, for a Church which had become *only* Roman would no longer be Catholic. And conversely, a lawful episcopate which would excommunicate the pope could never exist, since a Catholicity which renounces Rome would no longer be Catholic. Both are simultaneously included in the notion of Catholicity properly understood. The universal claim of the pope and the inherent limitation of this claim, which remains bound to the basic law of fulness, and so to the divine right of the bishops.

This opens up still another important vista on that question in which the problem of the word is crucially condensed, the question of the infallibility of the Church; or put another way, of the relation between episcopal (conciliar) and papal infallibility. It is not possible, within the framework of this study, to go into the details of this complicated controversy,[40] in which precision of thought has often been achieved only at the expense of reality. But we shall point out what light is shed on the question by what we have been saying.

It can be established that episcopal-conciliar infallibility, by its nature, can never legitimately conflict with papal infallibility. An "ecumenical" council which took sides against the pope, would thereby betray its non-ecumenicity, since after all a council held without or against the See of St. Peter is not ecumenical, ecumenicity depending essentially on the participation of Rome, the supreme apostolic see. The majority of the bishops has, from time immemorial in the Church, been determined not simply by the externally greater number, but by the "weight" of the sees. And there can be no number large enough to counterbalance the decisive weight of the See of St. Peter. Anything else would mean substituting some sort of profane arithmetic for the holy bond of tradition. To this extent a council is never an independent subject of infallibility, distinct from, or even against, the pope. For the pope is himself a bishop, *the* ecumenical bishop, without whom the episcopate would never have its full number, nor above all its "full weight", but would necessarily have to be judged "too light". Thus it is that the decrees of the pope are *ex sese* irreformable.[41]

---

[40] Cf. Th. Spácil, "Der Träger der kirchlichen Unfehlbarkeit", *Zeitschrift für katholische Theologie* 40 (1916), pp. 524–552. In the same periodical; against him: A. Straub, "Gibt es zwei unabhängige Träger der kirchlichen Unfehlbarkeit?" 42 (1918), pp. 254–300; cf. also H. van Laak, *Institutionum theologiae fundamentalis repetitorium* (Rome, 1921); W. Bartz, *Die lehrende Kirche. Ein Beitrag zur Ekklesiologie M. J. Scheebens* (Trier, 1959), esp. pp. 140ff.

[41] Dz. 1839.

On the other hand, since the pope is the ecumenical bishop he cannot and may not, by reason of his office, stand against the "ecumene". He is the sign of the true "ecumene" and it in turn is the sign which authenticates him. Precisely because of the inner nature of his infallibility, he needs the testimony of the "ecumene", of an episcopate which consists not of papal officials, shadows of himself, but of bishops in their own divine right, whose concrete "ecumene" visibly attests and fulfills his inner and essential "ecumene". Even after the definition of papal infallibility, indeed because of it, a council has its necessary and immutable meaning.

Let us finally turn once more to the religious-statistical formula "Roman Catholic" with which we started. Basically it reflects the entire complex of problems which we have gone through in the course of these considerations. In that it says "Catholic" it is distinguished from a Christianity based on Scripture alone, and instead acknowledges faith in the authority of the living word, *i.e.*, in the office of the apostolic succession. In that it says "Roman" it firmly refers this office to its centre, the office of the keys vested in the successor of St. Peter in the city consecrated by the blood of two apostles. By uniting the two to say "Roman Catholic" it expresses the pregnant dialectic between primacy and episcopate, neither of which exists without the other. A church which wished to be only "Catholic", having no part with Rome, would thereby lose its Catholicity. A church which, *per impossibile,* wished to be only Roman without being Catholic, would similarly deny herself and degenerate into a sect. "Roman" guarantees true Catholicity; actual Catholicity attests Rome's right.

But at the same time the formula expresses the twofold

breach running through the Church: the breach between "Catholicism" and the Christianity of the mere written word; the breach between Christianity based upon the Roman office of Peter, and Christianity severed from it. In both cases it is ultimately the "office" which causes the parting of the ways. Does this not recall in terrible fashion that quarrelling began even among Christ's disciples for the places to the right and to the left of the master, that is, for the offices in the coming messianic kingdom? And ought it not to recall to both sides the words of the Lord, that the greatest must be as the least, and the servant of all?[42] This is not to do away with the office; the mandate to Peter and the mandate to the apostles are not withdrawn. But it is a demand of ultimate urgency addressed both to those who, vested with the office, are preachers of the word, and to their listeners. To the former that they should strive to be in very truth *servi servorum Dei;* to the latter, not to refuse to be outwardly the "last" in order to know, in humble joy, that, precisely thus and not otherwise, they are first. Only if both – those in office and those without – seek the spirit of the Gospel in unconditional integrity can there be hope for a union of those who would never have been torn asunder without a denial of this spirit.

[42] Mark. 9:33ff. Mark. 10:35–45.

III

ON THE DIVINE RIGHT OF THE EPISCOPATE

Karl Rahner

1. Preliminary Remarks

THE theology of the relation between the papal primacy and
the episcopate is undoubtedly one part of ecclesiology which has
yet to find its final form. Even that degree of development
possible in today's circumstances has not yet been reached. It is of
course recognized that the Vatican Council could not treat this
question systematically and thoroughly, after defining the
universal and ordinary episcopal primacy of jurisdiction of the
pope, because of the break–up of the Council. And not all
questions about this relationship which arise in the practical life
of the Church can be solved by dogmatic ecclesiology, since
the concrete relationship between these two powers in the practical life of the Church cannot be unequivocally deduced from
the Church's dogmatic nature *iuris divini* alone. It is also a matter
of historical development, of practical experience, of *human* law
in the Church, and must be continually thought through and
regulated anew in her changing historical circumstances.

The plain fact that this concrete relationship has had a history
is clear proof that it lawfully can and will have a history in the
future as well, because the history of the Church will continue.
From this fact alone, it would be false and naïve to think,

consciously or unconsciously, that this relationship in the course of history has developed dogmatically, canonically and practically into its final form, which will now endure without any further change. If one were tacitly to assume, therefore, that even the slightest modification in this relationship (within the framework of the permanent *ius divinum,* of course) would amount to at least a secret attack either on this *ius divinum* or upon a form of the Church's *ius humanum* never to be improved upon, this would be to deny the basic truth that the Church is truly an historical thing. It would be to forget that the Church preserves and remains faithful to her Christ-given, permanent nature precisely by continually expressing it in a temporally conditioned form, in her *ius humanum* and in its practical application according to the needs of the time.

If the dogmatic theologian is not the only one called upon to consider this relationship in its concrete form, still we presume it will not be alleged that further dogmatic reflection on the nature of the Church and on the theological nature (that is, the divine right) of the relationship between primacy and episcopate has nothing more to contribute to the perennially necessary discussion about the form this relation takes in practice. This is the object of some of the dogmatic considerations that follow. They are not particularly systematic, nor do they pretend to exhaust the subject.[1]

According to defined Catholic doctrine, the pope personally possesses a full, immediate, ordinary and general episcopal primacy of jurisdiction over the whole Church and over her

---

[1] The reader is referred to the first part of this book for a fuller treatment of what will be repeated here only in brief.

every part and member, including the bishops.[1a] On the other hand it is definitive Catholic teaching (though not as yet defined in terms of such conscious clarity) that the episcopate exists of divine right[1b] in such a way that the pope, for all his jurisdictional primacy, cannot abolish it, that the bishops are not to be considered mere functionaries or representatives of the Roman Pontiff, that they have, rather, their own proper power to tend their flocks, not in the name of the pope, but in Christ's name and their own, and are therefore successors of the apostles by divine disposition. "The episcopate exists in virtue of the same divine institution on which the papacy rests; it too has its rights and duties, which the pope has neither the right nor the power to change. It is therefore a complete misunderstanding ... to suppose ... that the bishops are only instruments of the pope, officials of his without personal responsibility." "According to the constant teaching of the Catholic Church, as expressly declared also by the Vatican Council, the bishops are not mere instruments of the pope, not papal officials without responsibility of their own, but established by the Holy Spirit and taking the place of the apostles, as true shepherds they tend and rule the flocks entrusted to them ..." Thus the already quoted statement of the German episcopate of 1875, which enjoyed the express and solemn approbation of Pius IX.[2] If we compare these two statements on the episcopate and the papal primacy, both no doubt correct, we shall not be able to say that their compatibility is immediately evident, either in theory or in practice.

[1a] Dz. 1831; CJC, can. 218.
[1b] Dz. 960, 966, 1821, 1828.
[2] Cf. J. Neuner – H. Roos, *Der Glaube der Kirche in den Urkunden der Lehrverkündigung* (Regensburg, 1958), n. 388a.

Not in theory: it is not easy to understand how it is that a bishop has inalienable rights *iuris divini* which the pope cannot take from him, how it is that he governs his flock in the name of Christ and his own name, and not in the name of the pope, how it is that he is no mere functionary, when nowhere in our ecclesiology are we able to lay down within definable limits which rights[3] the episcopate as a whole, and hence the individual bishop, inalienably and irrevocably possesses; when the pope has undoubted right, immediately and in any given case, and without having to observe any judicial process, to intervene directly in any diocese and in any of its affairs, to appoint or to depose any bishop. Our question cannot be adequately answered by emphasizing that the pope can dispose of all these rights of the bishop, but that in fact he will never do so. It is not a question of the mere practical relations between the episcopate and the papal primacy, but of the basic legal relationship as such. Nor is it sufficient to point out that the pope naturally needs in his government of the universal Church some such local subordinates to whom he must grant a certain measure of authority, just as in an absolute monarchy or a radically totalitarian system, because without them he would simply be physically unable personally to carry on the government of the universal Church in all its detailed dispositions and arrangements.

Such a presentation of the case would imply that we were still considering the bishops as nothing more than functionaries, whose power was only a portion of the papal jurisdiction granted them by the pope. It cannot be denied that many Christians, judging more from the external appearance of the administrative

---

[3] Disregarding of course, the mere *"potestas ordinis"*.

practice of the Church than from dogmatic considerations, view the matter in this way. They regard the bishops as officials of the pope, the sole true ruler of the one Church, whose unity is conceived on the model of the modern state in which the only regions recognized are administrative districts. But that does not justify this view. I do not intend here and now to take up afresh the question why the appearance is false that the bishop is but the commissioned functionary of the pope, directing in the name and *ad nutum* of the pope a territorially limited administrative district, even though it is impossible to adduce a definite sum of rights reserved in every case to the bishop. For the fundamental answer to this problem the reader is referred to the first part of this book. Here I intend to supplement those considerations in certain respects.

2. Necessity and Precise Definition of the Question

First a comparison: a large part of the natural law of social behaviour will find its way, in a well ordered state, into the civil code and become positive law as well. But it is not to be expected *a priori* that the whole content of the natural law concerning social conduct, even obligations in justice, will expressly be defined in such a code of law. The same can be true in the Church. The divine right of the episcopate, which flows from the very essence of the Church, need not, for all that, already be expressed in its full development and with all desirable clarity in the explicit statements of our dogmatic theology about the Church, or in canon law. This right as a whole (despite possible individual abuses) is always present in the Church, of course, but as something which is lived. Nevertheless, it is not at all impossible that much which *de facto* happens in the relation, for example, between pope and bishops, is *ius divinum* though not explicitly recognized as such, and is therefore occasionally infringed, at least in individual cases, even given good will on both sides.

When we consult the average tract on ecclesiology for its doctrine on the *ius divinum* of the episcopate, which cannot be abolished even by the pope, we learn hardly anything beyond the fact that the episcopate is *iuris divini* and that the pope therefore cannot abolish it altogether. No doubt this is much too general an answer for us to take as an adequate and articulated account of the *ius divinum* of the episcopate, as if everything but the nominal existence of the bishops were therefore mere *ius humanum;* something which the pope could grant the bishops or withhold as he alone thought best; something normal to the Church only in certain exigencies of which the pope alone could definitively judge.

The existence of an episcopate without any definable essence would be absurd. If the episcopate exists of divine right, the episcopate must have an essence of divine right. Now this essence of divine right cannot reasonably be based on those powers alone which we refer to as the episcopal power of order. For if one be of the perfectly legitimate, though not certain, opinion that even a simple priest can at times, with the authorization of the pope, ordain priests; and if one share the view, by no means censurable even today, that the episcopate represents no new sacramental order superior to the priesthood,[4]

---

[4] This does not mean to imply that the author of this article shares this opinion. Quite the contrary. His conviction is that the Church, even as to *potestas ordinis,* can distribute the sacred powers present in her by the will of her Founder, in that measure which she finds appropriate at any

but is merely a hierarchical degree distinguished *iure divino* from the priesthood because of its powers of jurisdiction, then one can no longer specify what absolute difference there is, as to the power of order, between priest and bishop. Therefore the *ius divinum* which must be attributed to the essence of the episcopate and the existence of which is certain (and therefore cannot be made to depend on uncertain, conflicting opinions about the difference in the power of order between priest and bishop) must be sought also and above all in the power of jurisdiction. Even if, according to the common doctrine today, the bishop receives his power of jurisdiction from the pope, yet the power thus received is *iuris divini*, not a portion of the pope's own power delegated to the bishop. Rather, the pope, in appointing the individual bishop, gives him a share in the power of the whole episcopate *iuris divini* which was granted the Church by Christ. This the pope can and must impart to the individual bishop, but it does not follow that he could withhold it for

given time. The possibility of passing on "in doses" the powers inherent in a "perfect society" seems to the author to follow directly from the nature of such a society, even though we can point to no express declaration about it by the founder of this society. If therefore the Church today almost universally holds (which seems to be the case) that she gives the priest less *potestas ordinis* at his ordination than she does to the bishop at his consecration, (e. g. with respect to the consecration of bishops) then we can safely conclude that she does not *intend* to give the priest more *potestas ordinis*, and that, since she does not intend to, she does not do so. But since this question has not yet been settled among theologians, (and is probably still left open by the Apostolic Constitution of Pius XII, "*Sacramentum ordinis*"), the consideration above is justified as an "*argumentum ad hominem*" to show that the *ius divinum* of the episcopate cannot consist in the *potestas ordinis* alone – insofar as this thesis has to be defended at all against some imaginary opponent.

himself, (in which case, of course, the bishop would be a mere official of the pope).

But this only raises in more urgent fashion the problem of the content of this episcopal power of jurisdiction which belongs to the whole episcopate by divine right and which the pope cannot retain for himself. No doubt it must be possible to say more about this content than theological textbooks and canon law expressly state. Much (not all!) that bishops do as a matter of course and that is also permitted by the Holy See as a matter of course is not mere *de facto* custom, something the pope could as well withdraw from the bishops, or has to give them merely because an official must have certain permanent powers if he is not to be useless, but is *iuris divini,* even when not explicitly so conceived. This is not to say (as has already been emphasized above) that concrete, definitely fixed individual rights of an *individual* bishop as an individual must be *iuris divini* in such a way that the pope could not deprive the bishop of one of these particular rights. Such a claim would be of no practical use and would really be senseless, because it could only fortify, and provide some content for, the episcopal jurisdiction if the bishop were declared legally irremovable. But since this is impossible, any attempt to define the content of the *ius divinum* in the bishops' jurisdiction by listing inalienable particular rights is futile from the start.

Nevertheless this is not to say that, apart from its general origin, the *ius divinum* of the bishop is impossible to define. Though the attempt to fix the material limits of the rights of the papacy and the episcopate is not feasible for the reasons indicated above, and though we cannot ascertain a residue of particular episcopal jurisdictional rights which escape papal supremacy, nevertheless the inalienable episcopal *ius divinum* need not be thought void of any real content.

3. The ius divinum *of the whole Episcopate* is the Material and Cognitive Ground of the ius divinum *of Individual Bishops*

Its exact definition must proceed on the one hand from the nature of the universal Church, and on the other from the nature of the episcopate as a college (the successor of the apostolic college, which as a college takes precedence over the individual apostles and their powers, and is not merely the sum of the individual apostles and their powers).

The first point of departure is obvious: the nature of the Church is always the permanent foundation of the nature of her governmental powers, even though we cannot deduce, from any abstract concept of the nature of the Church alone, her exact juridical structure, which is at least in part an additional positive institution of Christ, so that an exact concept of the Church entails some knowledge of her juridical constitution, of the authorities that govern her, and of their rights and duties. Yet recourse to the theological nature of the Church which underlies her juridical structure is always advisable, even necessary, if one is seeking an accurate notion of her organs of government.

But the second approach mentioned above is the decisive one in our case. The answer to the problem of the *ius divinum* of the individual bishop lies in the *ius divinum* of the universal episcopate. To understand our point, we must remember that the papal power over the individual bishop, even to the point of deposing him, cannot and may not, by a simple extension, be exercised over the universal episcopate; that, therefore, the pope's rights over the universal episcopate are not the mere sum of his rights over the individual bishops. Therefore the papal rights over the individual bishop must be exercised in such a way that the divine right of the universal episcopate as a college is not, in effect, abolished or its nature threatened. The fact that a particular limitation of a bishop's episcopal rights by the pope happens to be canonically and dogmatically legitimate in a particular case, does not at all imply that the same limitation can by divine right be imposed on the rights of the universal episcopate. Because the universal episcopate, as the apostolic college living on in history, has *qua* college inalienable rights and duties *iuris divini,* the pope is obliged to take care, lest some of his measures, legitimate when imposed on an individual bishop, infringe the original right of the universal episcopate – for example, if the sum total of such measures taken against many bishops should make the rights (and duties) of the universal episcopate illusory in practice, or reduce them to a dimension where they might survive in practice, but without any clear juridical status.

Even if it cannot be said that the pope has only those rights over individual bishops which he has over the universal episcopate as such, neither can one conversely conclude from the papal right over the individual bishop to the existence of that same right over the bishops as a whole. A simple example, obvious and familiar: the pope could remove a particular bishop and install an apostolic vicar or administrator, that is, a papal official, in his place. Nobody can conclude from this that he could do this with all the bishops at one time. This would amount to abolishing the episcopate itself, which the pope cannot do. One can even go so far as to say that the full participation of a bishop in the rights and duties of the universal episcopate is *de iure* to be presumed, so that the contrary, in the case of a particular bishop or a particular measure, must be proved, even though the burden of proof and the actual proof is left to the conscience of the pope, against whom the individual bishop has no legal recourse. Therefore, *iuris divini,* the rights of the universal episcopate can be taken from an individual bishop only to the extent which the concrete circumstances show to be lawful and equitable.

But with this the problem is not solved, only transferred. The problem of the content of any single bishop's divinely given jurisdictional power becomes the problem of the jurisdiction of the episcopate as a whole. And, according to the history of the Church, which, on the whole, may be taken as a guide to what is legitimate, the divine right of the episcopate is not (materially, at least) bound to any absolutely fixed form as its realization in the concrete. Then again, the episcopate is obviously the subject of these divine rights only insofar as it is unified in the bishop of Rome, that is, it is not really a subject of rights as a college *vis-à-vis* the pope, but in unity with him.

But subject to these presuppositions and qualifications, the question can and must be put whether and how the content of the episcopate's rights *iuris divini* can be more precisely defined. The problem is a difficult one, one that theology to date can hardly claim to have properly posed, much less adequately answered. Our attempt here to pose the question more accurately and (as far as possible) to answer it can only be modest and fragmentary.

4. The Theological Nature of
the College of Apostles

We shall take as our point of departure a principle which will not be disputed, that the episcopate as a whole is the successor of the apostolic college. An individual bishop is not the successor of an individual apostle. He is only in the line of succession from an apostle insofar as he belongs to the Church's episcopate, which in turn, as a body, succeeds the corporate apostolic college. Theology emphasizes this point in the process of giving a detailed definition of "apostolic succession", or when it asks why an individual bishop is not automatically infallible though he is a successor of the apostles to whom theology ascribes infallibility, primarily as a body but also in their individual capacity. It is of paramount importance firmly to grasp the point that the apostolic college as a genuine *corporate body* holds the authority in the Church; and that the apostles as individuals[5] did not first receive

---

[5] This need not exclude an apostle's having certain authority, powers, charismata, etc. as an "individual" as well. We cannot go into this point here. Suffice it to say, first of all, that the point made in the text does not exclude a grant of such personal powers and privileges through a positive disposition of Christ. Nor is it, secondly, at all unthinkable that because of the function of the college of apostles in the "Apostolic Church" (cf. Karl Rahner, *Inspiration in the Bible,* New York 1961, p. 42–47, in a specifically theological sense of the term referring to the Church's beginnings as decisive and normative for all future times, never subject to revision) extraordinary powers belonged also to the individual apostle as such (even though they belong to him because of his membership in this college as the college of the Apostolic Church). These powers were not passed on to later bishops as members of the governing body of the later Church. Thirdly, the notion of membership in a college does not exclude but rather includes (at least with certain colleges) the possibility of rights and duties of the individual members as such deriving from the

their distinct powers from Christ separately and then afterwards bind themselves together to form a college. The ontological and juridical relationship is the other way round: Jesus founds a college. In it the apostles have power[6] insofar and only insofar as they are members of this college and are acting as such. From any other point of view it is impossible to understand how Peter can appear from the beginning as head of the apostolic college. If each apostle were first of all an individually authorized representative of Christ, then no subordination of the apostles to Peter (or rather, no subordination of the individual apostles to a college with Peter at its head) would ever be possible. The individual apostle would then have immediately from Christ an authority of such a kind that he would not possess it *qua* member of the college. He could not be held accountable to Peter or to the college, but only to Christ, the direct source of his authority.

Once again we are faced with the dilemma which in the case of the relationship between the primacy and the episcopate can

---

college, though the primary and basic function of a member of the college can only be exercised in an act of the whole body. A member of parliament can, for example, only legislate validly insofar as parliament itself (and he in it) legislates. But his function as a member of such a body may imply a right which he as an individual enjoys, his immunity, for example. In this sense it is possible that powers and rights of individual apostles as such did flow from their membership in the collegiate body of apostles which they could exercise as individuals, and which rights later passed to individual bishops, because and if they did not arise solely from the situation of the Church being the Apostolic Church. But even those rights and powers belonging to the apostles as individuals must have flowed ultimately from their membership in the college of apostles as such.

[6] The power meant here is the basic power that makes an apostle an apostle.

be resolved only by recognizing the college as such to be the prior entity, not subseqently composed of individuals already possessed of their own authority before entering the college; and that the primacy of the pope is a primacy *within* and not *vis-à-vis* this college. If the apostles had their authority first of all as individuals, they could hold this authority only by a mandate which Christ had given to them as individuals, or by a mandate from Peter. In the first case, they would no longer be subject to Peter; in the second, they would be apostles of Peter, not of Christ.[7] Only if Christ founds a college which as such has an authoritative head and yet as such possesses real power deriving from himself, so that from the outset Peter can never be thought of without the other apostles, nor the college without Peter, is an apostle really an apostle of Christ, come of Christ and of Christ's own mission. And yet he is such an apostle only within the college and consequently under Peter, because this college, according to Scripture once again, was set up by Christ with one part subordinate to the other. It did not autonomously choose this structure for itself. Such a procedure would only be conceivable if the apostles had each his own authority as an individual, whether from Christ or from the Church. But at best this would give the apostles as a college an

[7] To say that Christ bestows on each individual apostle his authority, but with the command to use it (under pain of invalidating his act) in subordination to Peter, is objectively correct. But this only circumvents the problem instead of answering it. How can a person be given an authority which is completely at the disposal of a third person, without this authority thereby being a delegated authority originally vested in this third person? However positive the institution of a right may be, the logic and facts of the case simply do not permit just any "combination". Rights cannot be granted and taken away at the same time.

organization that could be altered at will, and it would then be open to question *why* the individual apostles had to unite in a college at all.

To approach the problem from another angle: *non enim plura secundum se uniuntur*. A real unity is prior to its parts, not made up out of them as parts. If the individual apostles together founded a college according to their own notions, then it would be dependent on their will, and the individuals could not be dependent on Peter *iuris divini*. Or if unity originated with Peter as its proper and active cause (not only its representative, who realizes in the life of the Church the unity which already exists), then *he* would be affiliating a college to himself to be *his* agent, and its members would receive a power dependent upon him. (This is quite a different thing from having no power except insofar as they remain dependent on him; in the first case Peter would be the source of power, in the second he is the prerequisite for its lawful possession and exercise.) They would be his functionaries, entrusted with that portion of his own power which he thought fit to give them. As both these hypotheses break down, our only recourse is to conclude that what Christ founded was precisely a college from the outset, in which the individual apostle has an authority he derives from Christ because Christ endowed the college as such with its authority, and that Peter has his unique authority insofar as he is constituted head of this college from the outset.

Another indication that the apostles, in the thought of Jesus, were to be a college from the beginning is their function of tangibly representing the unity of the New Israel, mystically composed of twelve tribes. There is, accordingly, no mention in the New Testament of functions belonging to one apostle rather than another, such as the administration of a particular territory (the *"divisio apostolorum"* is a typically late and apocryphal piece). Wherever the apostles appear on the scene after Pentecost it is always as a collegiate body.[7a] Where individual apostles (even Peter) emerge from the college and come into view they act by commission of the college; wherever they go, they go as representatives of the college (*e.g.,* Samaria). This permits us to say without hesitation: Peter is Peter, insofar as he is head of this college, *i.e.,* he has his position in the Church as vicar of the master of the household to the extent that he is head of the apostolic college. This does not mean, of course, that he is democratically commissioned from below to represent the college, as though the organization already had the full legal capacity to act, and then, for practical reasons, chose to act through a single head. The apostolic college itself exists inasmuch as and because it possesses its head, and this head is appointed by Christ. But equally the head is furnished with his powers by Christ insofar as he is appointed head. Ontologically and juridically, then, the apostolic college with Peter at its head forms one entity. The college cannot exist without Peter, nor he without it. One could say that Peter is the divinely ordained head of the Church insofar as he is head of the apostolic college, which he rules while ruling the Church with it. "With it", not "through it". Here again, without having made much progress, we meet the basic logical and juridical problem in the Church's constitution. She is ruled by a *college,* without its head thereby becoming the mere elected representative of the college; the head truly

[7a] Acts 15; Gal. 2:1–10; Acts 1:13ff.; 2:42; 4:33; 5:2; 5:12; 5:18, 29, 40; 6:2; 8:1, 14; 9:27; 11:1; 15:6, 22, 23.

rules the college, without the college thereby becoming his mere executive organ.

This relationship is undoubtedly one which cannot be adequately reduced to legal terms. No axiomatic juridical principle can be laid down capable of materially governing the relationship between Peter and the other apostles once and for all, and of marking off their respective spheres of competence.[8] Such a state of affairs, which would, in the long run, prove the undoing of any secular body, flows from that unique relationship between whole and part peculiar to the Church.[9] It has proved juridically durable in the course of history because an absolute conflict between these two mutually restrictive elements of the Church's governing body, or a complete elimination of one by the other, is prevented by a supra–juridical authority, the assistance of the Holy Ghost.

The structure of the Church rests essentially on something

---

[8] The difficulty arises from the fact fact that we have a real ecclesiastical entity on each side only insofar as both sides are united to make up the one apostolic college under Peter, and that nonetheless, we can always wonder how the two are juridically related "to one another", because both Peter and the other apostles are real persons, free agents with their own ideas, who act upon one another. But precisely this right to reciprocal activity, which does exist, must be derived from the nature of their unity among one another. It is not something which the two parts have independently of and prior to this unity. In a purely physical structure there is no difficulty in understanding that the norm of one part's "activity" is the function it has in the whole. It is when this "part" is a conscious, free, responsible person, that we find it hard to grasp this clearly. From the unity of the personal agent, we almost automatically conclude to a "right" he has independent of and prior to the collegiate unity, and which thus governs his relationship to the college.

[9] Cf. above, p. 7.

supra-institutional, on the Nomos of the Spirit, which cannot and will not adequately be translated into institutional terms.[10] Yet this very fact makes it possible to ascertain more precisely the content of the authority of the whole apostolic college, and thus of the individual apostles. The college rules the Church. But this means that the apostles' function in the universal Church is an active one. They are not merely executive agents of Peter, doing his will. Precisely because within the college each apostle actively co-governs the universal Church as such, it is *a priori* impossible for any sphere to be reserved to him alone, whether territorially, materially or departmentally, beyond the governmental reach of the apostolic college or of Peter. But for this reason also each individual apostle has an active function of his own which originates with him and the exercise of which he cannot give up. How he brings this activity into operation in such a manner that (explicitly or implicitly) it becomes the activity of the whole college and thereby legitimate in the eyes of the Church, is not something to be regulated by canons, but is left to the apostle's own judgment, even with respect to its harmony with the activity of Peter and the other apostles. He knows, as it were, only two things: that he is obliged to be constantly active, exercising an initiative and responsibility which cannot be transferred to others or deduced from directives of theirs; and that the Holy Spirit, not some fixed rule setting limits to his competence, will see to it that this responsible initiative, which is both his right and his duty, will have the abiding influence

---

[10] This has its analogy in profane matters. No set of positive propositions for instance, can adequately express the natural law or replace and render superfluous formal principles such as equity, which can never be translated completely into the form of propositions.

and effect which the situation requires, at least on the whole and in the long run.

Such initiative can, from the nature of the college and its authority as both a unity and a composite thing, take either of two forms. Either an apostle tries to win the college for his line of action (though there is no legal procedure available to him for this purpose, since such a thing would destroy the supra-legal unity of the college and the full juridical power of its head) or he may represent the college where, so far as practical activity is concerned, it is not physically present but can be so.

The initiative of the individual apostle in regard to the college (without which a college as an acting body is unthinkable, since it can really act only in and through physical persons) implies in the other members a duty to listen, a basic readiness to remain open to such initiative. On the one hand, it is more fitting to qualify this duty as moral rather than legal, because the original subject of rights in the Church is the college as a whole, and so this duty has no corresponding concrete person to judge of its neglect or fulfilment, distinct from the body itself which owes this duty. On the other hand, this duty is legal insofar as it is an element necessarily implied in the rights each apostle has as an active member of the college. Nor is this duty limited depart-mentally, insofar as it signifies active participation in the authority of the one ruling college in the Church. Each apostle is (always within the college) competent in the entire government of the whole Church. He bears the whole burden together with Peter, he concerns himself with the whole Church in all her labours and necessities. Such authority may, of course, have a local objective. Peter and John travel to Samaria as represent-atives of the whole college, as Acts 8, 14 explicitly attests. Such a conception is quite unobjectionable from the point of view of the Church's teaching concerning the position of Peter. The apostolic college is not a body above Peter, it is itself only with him as its active head. In this capacity it commissions Peter to go to Samaria. Peter's whole function is to be head of the college — Peter, the keeper of the keys. His function is not territorial or departmental. He is not pope because he receives some commission from the apostolic college to work in Samaria or in Rome, but because he, with the college and as its head, commissions others and so also himself with a special function — as giving the special function, not receiving it. All these primatial rights are rights of the head of the college as such. They are based on the existence of the college, not as though given by the college conceived as a pre-existing thing capable of its own activity (to stress our point once again), but as rights which would cease really to exist unless the college existed in its entirety, acting as a unit with Peter, and founded as such by Christ. Hence it is most significant and altogether appropriate that the apostles act as a college, and do not postpone the realization of their apostolic character until (as later legends have it) they come to divide the world among themselves. They had no need to be predecessors of the bishops as rulers of the Church in certain restricted territories, nor were they such.

5. The College of Bishops as Successor of the Apostolic College

With this in mind, then, let us investigate more closely the thesis that the episcopate is the successor of the apostolic college.

6*

83

a) Priority of the College of Bishops over the Individual Bishops

The college of bishops, as successsor of the apostolic college, takes priority over the individual bishops, their rights and responsibilities. The college of bishops is neither a logical sum of the individual bishops in the mind of some external observer, nor is it their subsequent incorporation, effected either by the bishops themselves or by the pope. The bishops' college is the primary entity, successor to the apostolic college, having in the pope its pre-ordained head, without whom it cannot be conceived, as the head of which alone the pope can be pope.

This follows first of all from the truth that the Church (even as visibly constituted) is primarily *one* (although, while one, she contains a basic pluralism in the differentiation of her members). And she is one, not merely through the activity of the individual faithful or individual churches (to which the nature of the Church is prior), as though these had created her unity by forming themselves into an association, but because she was originally founded as one and always so exists. And this holds even in the social and juridical order, because without such an order the Church does not exist. But if unity is prior and primordial, then the college of bishops is prior to the individual bishops, unless this unity is to be manifested only in the pope, which cannot be true because then the episcopate would not be of divine right.

That the primary unity of the episcopate takes precedence over the individual bishops and their power follows also from the fact that the episcopate succeeds the apostolic college, which, as a unity, ranks before the plurality of the individual apostles, as we have shown.

Our contention can also be clarified by another consideration. According to the CJC a council has supreme authority in the

Church. This principle must be *iuris divini,* for if it were human law in the Church, it would mean a legal curtailment of the divine right of the pope (of whom the same thing is said) and/or imply a concession on the pope's part. But neither can be correct, for the pope cannot relinquish the rights he has *iure divino,* and one could not say that a council had supreme authority in the Church, if it had this authority from the pope and therefore subject to revocation.

But if the council, being summoned by the pope, were nothing more than the purely conceptual sum of the individual bishops as such, then a council could never be termed the highest and sovereign subject of power in the Church. For the individual bishops as such cannot have this plenitude of power. The aggregation of individual bishops as such could not deprive the individual bishop of his own proper power, since it cannot curtail the power of those individuals by whose free decision, *ex supposito,* it has its very existence. The council as such, then, could have a sovereign power over the individual bishop, if at all, only in and through the power of the pope. But then, once more, the council could only be conceived as an organ of the pope. Its power would be, at best, part of the pope's power as such, since he, in delegating it, chooses to share it with the council; or else the council would be only the auxiliary and advisory organ of the pope. But by no means could one say that the council had supreme power in the Church. The council could not have such a supreme power if the pope not only called it and presided over it,[11] but also had to constitute it a subject of this power which

---

[11] This does not contradict the supreme power of the council, because that which here assembles in council, the episcopal college which always had this supreme power, has the pope as its summit.

previously did not exist. Then this subject could only be the subject of that power which the pope gives as his own. It would then be the subject of a power comprehended, supported and conditioned by the power of the pope insofar as he is distinct from the council and deals with it as such. A power of this description could hardly be called supreme.

We remain caught in this dilemma as long as we fail to realize that the college of bishops always exists as such in the Church and does not first come into being when the bishops gather in council, and that the college of bishops as such is always the subject of the *suprema potestas in Ecclesia,* even though this *potestas in Ecclesia* has remained, as it were, on a para-canonical level so far as our present canon law is concerned. Such a conception does not restrict or threaten the papal primacy, since the college of bishops always includes the pope as its head, without which it could not exist at all. It is the council itself that acts when the pope acts, by reason of his supreme jurisdiction, because the pope, precisely when he acts *ex sese,* acts not as a private person but as pope, that is, as head of a college of bishops *iuris divini.* In other words, in the canonical conception of the nature of the council as subject of the supreme power in the Church, the same thing is implicitly declared to be true of the college of bishops.[12] This leads, however, to the conclusion that the college of bishops, as such, exists as the supreme subject of governmental power in

---

[12] This is stated quite explicitly, by the way, in the doctrine on the *ordinary* magisterium of the college of bishops, for this magisterium of the episcopate as a whole possesses, according to the explicit teaching of all ecclesiologists, the same teaching authority as the extraordinary magisterium of a council. Only the manner of its exercise is different, but not its subject, competence or binding force.

the universal Church prior to the individual bishop as such. The individual bishop is primarily a member of the universal episcopate as the collegiate[13] ruling body of the Church, which *iure divino* finds in the pope its permanent unity and the possibility of lasting concrete activity.

b) Possible Objections

Against the proposed thesis the objection could be raised that the bishops were from the very beginning so much governors of territorially delimited communities that for this reason alone it seems improbable that they were originally conceived as a college, and that thus their college could have been the successor of the apostolic college. In other words, since the bishops did not first appear as a college, they cannot have been intended to form a college in succession to the apostolic college. And this function cannot, therefore, have been their primary one.

This objection, it must be pointed out first of all, is not directed against our thesis alone as proposed above, but against the general Catholic teaching that the bishops are the successors of the apostles. We can dispense, therefore, with a detailed rebuttal of the objection, recalling only what every ecclesiology has to say about the bishops as successors of the apostles. It

---

[13] The term "collegiate" does not, of course, in any way imply that the pope is only a *primus inter pares,* who elect him as an official of theirs. But it does mean that the subject of the supreme power in the Church is composed of many physical persons. If this were fundamentally impossible, then it would be equally impossible and false for the council to be the subject of supreme power in the Church. This latter, however, is not false, but true. And therefore it is true that the Church has, in the episcopate as a whole a collegiate "summit". This does not exclude the college itself having a personal summit in the pope.

suffices here to point out that from the beginning of the second century we find everywhere in the Church the monarchical episcopate, and the idea that these bishops derive their office and their authority "in apostolic succession" from the apostles. Or, to look at the question another way, if Christ's community was to be governed, according to his will, by the apostolic college united under Peter, if the Church was to last until the end of time, then this apostolic college *must* have a successor. But there is no institution to be seen in the ancient Church which could even lay claim to such a succession except the episcopal body. This succession must then be found in them.

The fact that this same argument is used for the successors of Peter is another sign of its pertinence for understanding the Catholic Church. While today there are a good many Protestant exegetes who admit a primacy of some sort during the lifetime of Peter, but deny that this institution must in principle have continued on in the Church even after the death (or departure) of Peter (from Jerusalem), Catholic ecclesiology is firmly convinced that (even without an explicit testimony from the lips of Jesus) the function of Peter must have continued in the Church. But then the same must be said of the apostolic college. But then this college as such must continue, and since one cannot seriously maintain that the individual apostle had an official, regular function in the Church independent of, and prior to, his membership in the college of the Twelve, there must be a permanent successor in the Church for this college. But this implies not only the general thesis about the bishops as the successors of the apostles, but also the more precise interpretation which we have given to this doctrine. Even at the risk of displaying his ignorance the author must say that he knows of no work in recent literature which systematically treats the question of the exact relation between the territorially limited power of the individual bishop, and his membership in the episcopal college. The only exception known to me is a contribution from Spain, by Bernardo Monsegú.[14]

A detailed theological discussion of this article is not possible here. We should like only to make one point. Insofar as this work (the title of which poses the very problem we have treated here, and which does attempt its treatment), comes to a negative conclusion which contradicts the view we propose, it strikes us as unsound. It tacitly assumes that the co-optation of an individual into the episcopal college by the pope is impossible. Thus when the pope, according to the common teaching today, bestows the episcopal power on an individual bishop (as the cause and not merely the condition of the episcopal powers), then this could only be understood to mean that the primary, indeed only, object of the papal act was the bestowal of the territorially limited episcopal powers as such, and that membership in the episcopal college was a purely secondary consequence of his installation as ruler of a diocese.

But why should the head of a college not have the power to receive someone into that college? And why could the primary object of the installation of a bishop, its ultimate theological signification, not be such a co-optation into the college? It makes no difference that this act is usually described by its effect on the territorially limited episcopal powers. If the two things (mem-

[14] B. Monsegú, "Los obispos son sucesores de los Apóstoles directos inmediatamente como miembros del colegio, o más bien en cuanto personalmente consagrados o investidos de su oficio? XVI *Semana Española de Teología* (Sept. 17–22, 1956), (Madrid, 1957), p. 217–247.

bership in the episcopal college and the territorially limited episcopal office) are necessarily connected — at least according to present canon law and in the cases we here have in mind — then one can describe or designate the whole act according to either aspect. The mere fact that the territorial and not the collegiate aspect of the whole act of investiture occupies the foreground in the average canonical, religious and theological consciousness is no unequivocal indication of how these two things are objectively related to one another.[15]

We have so far always had in mind, in this whole question, "the normal bishop", that is, one who not only possesses the power of order through episcopal consecration, but also the power of jurisdiction over a certain diocese. This is the type we have studied, and considered as a member of the college of bishops. But there are others possessed of episcopal orders (because of the validity of their episcopal consecration) who, as heretics and schismatics, are not, according to the teaching of the Church, members of the Church (in the full sense); still less, then, can they be members of the college of bishops, the Catholic Church's supreme governing body. This being so, it is clear, on the one hand, that we have been correct up to now in looking on the power of jurisdiction over a part of the Catholic Church, in the full sense of "Catholic Church", as a condition, a sign, a part, and a consequence of membership in the college of bishops.

[15] We have the same kind of discrepancy between objective order and subjective emphasis in relation to two such elements, in the question whether the bishop of Rome is primarily bishop of Rome and therefore pope, or first pope and in addition also bishop of Rome, (even granting in the second case that the office of bishop is a condition and sign of possessing the primatial power in the whole Church).

But there remains, on the other hand, the question whether those Catholic bishops who are within the body of the Church but who do not rule any diocese of their own, are to be considered members of the college of bishops (that is, the college of bishops in the theological sense, as the supreme ruling body in the Church, not as the sum total of "bishops"). These bishops certainly cannot be regarded in the same way as those who through heresy or schism are separated from the one Church of Peter, because they are certainly full members of the Church. Yet they are hardly members of the college of bishops in the same sense as the *ordinarii loci*.

Membership of the supreme governing body of the Church entails the primary consequence that the apostles send one to "Samaria", that is, as a member of the supreme body there, to represent it by undertaking responsibility for a particular territory. And this definitely cannot be said of an auxiliary bishop. On the other hand, it follows from our considerations that it is not in principle impossible to belong to a college without having any authority or rôle to play apart from the college's own. This holds good in the case of the Church. One can certainly belong to the supreme governing body of the Church without possessing jurisdiction over any particular territory. There are ordinaries, in episcopal orders and otherwise, whose jurisdiction is personal. The question is thus not easy to answer. Perhaps we can say for the present that such bishops belong to the episcopal college by reason of their power of order — provided that we do not envisage this power as purely individualistic, but see it instead as part of the one episcopal power the proper subject of which is precisely the college of bishops under the pope. This can be done even if one grants that, because of the validity of their sacraments, there are real bishops outside the Church (a point we cannot go into here). Besides, it is not *a priori* impossible that the Church considers auxiliary bishops to be members of the college on the grounds of some function beyond the mere power of order, even though they are able to exercise that function only within the college as such and in respect of the college. *If* the Church can call an auxiliary bishop to a general council as a voting member — something which she can do, and which she provides for[16] — then it is not inconceivable that she tacitly regards an auxiliary bishop as a co-governing member of the college even outside a council; and this even though she does not entrust to him, on the grounds of this function in the college, a special function of his own, as she normally does in making a man a local ordinary.

c) The Subject(s) of Infallible Teaching Authority

The knowledgeable reader has probably noticed before now that our remarks about the relation between pope and episcopate touch upon a matter which is treated in ecclesiology as the question whether there are *two* inadequately distinct subjects of the magisterium in the Church, that is, the pope himself and the council under the pope, or only one, that is, the pope, so that he alone is the subject of active infallibility directly support-ed by the divine assistance, the council being only indirectly a subject of active infallibility insofar as the bishops in council, concurring with the pope, participate in the papal infallibility. This question, as is well known, is still controverted among theologians, and was expressly left open at the First Vatican

[16] Cf. J. Hamer, "Note sur la collégialité épiscopale", *Revue des Sciences Philosophiques et Théologiques* 44 (1960), p. 40–50.

Council (when, however, a "papal" theologian of the stature of Gasser considered the papal view "regrettable"[16a]). What we have been trying to say up to now can perhaps be clarified if we briefly relate it to this controversy.

First of all, it is remarkable that this controversy is only discussed under the heading of conciliar and papal infallibility. It is easy enough to see, however, that the basic question here is that of the general relation of the episcopal college to the pope, with all its rights and powers. The basic question underlying this controversy should be discussed and settled under the heading of the Church's fundamental constitution. One society can contain only one supreme authority; a double supreme authority seems a metaphysical absurdity from the outset (even with the qualification that these "two" powers are only inadequately distinct). Two supreme powers (powers, that is, from which there is no appeal to a higher court in this world), if they are really two, can only rule two distinct bodies. The two may be associated, but never really united, without the dual sovereignty ceasing to exist. When one considers as well the certain fact that in the Church only the supreme governing power (which includes the magisterium) can enjoy infallibility, and further, that a mediate, derivative and yet active infallibility, for this and other reasons (as Gasser too emphasized) amounts to a contradiction in terms, one is led to the inescapable conclusion that the papal theory, in insisting that there can be only one infallible authority in the Church, is quite correct. It has, as Salaverri[17] stresses, the "speculative" arguments on its side. It

---

[16a] Mansi 52, 1216.
[17] Patres S. J. Facultatum theologicarum in Hispania professores, *Sacrae Theologiae Summa I*⁴ (Madrid, 1958), p. 713, n. 640.

is impossible to speak of two infallibilities and therefore of two supreme teaching authorities and consequently of two supreme subjects of power in the Church. Whether one likes it or not, this would amount to denying the real unity of the Church, or to recognizing in one of the powers a merely nominal supremacy.

But at the same time we know from positive sources that the council too has an active infallibility, that in Council the bishops together with the pope are *judges* in matters of faith and not simply advisers to the pope or merely the first to express their assent to a papal decision which the pope has reached independently, something which would not transcend the "hearing" or passive infallibility possessed by all members of the hearing Church. Past councils, it must be admitted, never considered themselves to be mere sounding boards or "amplifiers" for papal infallibility. It would be absurd to envisage the early councils thus and no less absurd in the case of the later ones, even where no more doubts existed about the supreme papal primacy of jurisdiction and so about the pope's supreme magisterium. Many theologians,[18] even to the present day, point out that the promise of Christ to the apostolic college seems to signify an *immediate* divine assistance for the apostolic college as such,[18a] so that this apostolic college must be infallible directly, not "derivatively" from Peter. But if the pope (according to the promise to Peter) and the episcopal college as such (as united, of course, under its petrine head) are both infallible through immediate divine

---

[18] Cf. J. Salaverri, *Sacrae Theol. Summa* I , p. 713 ff., n. 641 ff. (and p. 686 ff., n. 561 ff.).

[18a] Matt. 18:18; 28:18–20; Mark 16:15; John 14:16; 17:26; 20:21; cf. Matt. 10:40; Luke 10:16.

assistance, then do we not after all have two supreme authorities in the Church, even if they are stated to be only inadequately distinct? It is precisely this dualism that is impossible. The dilemma seems inescapable. No wonder there has been no agreement on this question to this day.

The question to ask at this point is the following: Is the tacit assumption made by both sides correct, the assumption that the infallibility of the pope when he defines "alone" is in no way also the infallibility of the college of bishops? Grant the assumption, and either the pope alone must possess the immediate active infallibility (if there can be only one in the Church) or, if the council is also immediately infallible, then there must actually be two subjects of the infallible teaching authority, since the pope is also infallible "without" the council or the episcopal college. But the question is: Can the dilemma be judiciously avoided altogether by conceiving only one subject of supreme power from the start — the college of bishops united under the pope as its head, so that an act of the pope "alone" and an act of the council are only different forms and modes of the activity of this one subject of supreme ecclesiastical authority, but need not be derived from two different subjects? It is generally conceded that in the act of a council, and that as such, the act of the pope is always included. The terminology which speaks of papal "approbation" of conciliar decrees is to this extent unfortunate. This "approbation" is, after all, an intrinsic element of the conciliar decree itself, not the adventitious decree of a different authority, conceived as a check on the college, supervening from without as a condition for the validity of a decree, already fully constituted, of the council as a subject apart. The "approbation" is rather to be conceived as a constitutive element of the college

95

itself. But can we say conversely that the episcopal college with its authority and its act (if not formally as concentrated in council) is included in the pope, in his authority and his act, so that when the pope acts "alone" he still acts *as* head of the episcopal college, and his act is also the act of the college?

If this question may be answered in the affirmative, then it is clear without more ado that there is only *one* subject of infallibility in the Church and that nevertheless the council as such possesses an immediate active infallibility. That has been our answer, and therefore we feel we have superseded the controversy. Of course this thesis of a mutual rather than unilateral inclusion of papacy and fully constituted episcopal college would need to be established more in detail than we have done here. But it is clear that, fundamentally and quite in general, it does not involve any contradiction for an individual physical person to posit the act of a collegiate moral person without the other physical members' being required to posit the act physically with him. It is also clear that such a possibility is not limited to the case where the members of the college delegate this person to act in the name of the college. The appointment of a physical person to represent a legal person can be conceived as happening in the most various ways (by God, by the nature of the case, etc.). It can quite definitely be conceived in such a way that the body represented cannot itself reject the appointment (consider, for example, Adam's representation of the human race, in many interpretations of original sin). Such a representation of the college by an individual physical person, effected by a third party and not subject to repudiation by the college, can, in its precise content and powers and without its act ceasing to be an act of the college, be such that in a very real sense one could call this act the act of this physical person "alone", if only because the college cannot annul it. Such an interpretation of the word "alone" does ample justice to the Vatican Council's *"ex sese"* and *"non ex consensu"* of the Church. We have already shown that actually such a papal act occurs as the act of the episcopal college in more than a legalistic sense, that actually (without prejudice to the primatial rights of the papacy as defined by the Vatican Council) the papal act always expresses the reality and initiative of the episcopate in a variety of ways, even though the two parties are not two different juridical entities in the sense that the episcopate as a separate juridical entity could take legal proceedings against the pope in defence of its rights. The fact that these two concepts mutually include each other does not of course mean that they are related to each other in exactly the same way.

When therefore the pope defines sometimes "alone" and sometimes together with the council, it is not a question of two acts of different subjects, but of two different procedures of one and the same subject, which differ only in the circumstance that in the one case the one moral subject is "dispersed throughout the world", and in the other is assembled in one place, where the co-operation and fraternity of the members of the college with the head is more clearly manifested. For a better grasp of this point it will be well to reconsider the "ordinary magisterium". It too has only one subject, the unit comprised by the college with the pope as its head; it can also act when "dispersed" over the earth. Its activity too can assume concrete form in a special act of the pope, so that the question has arisen whether and in what circumstances such a papal act (though not a solemn definition) possesses the infallibility proper to the "ordinary magisterium".[19]

The relationship between the function of the pope (Peter) as head of the episcopal (apostolic) college, and the powers ascribed to him as head of the Church by the Vatican Council (universal, supreme, episcopal, immediate, sovereign power over the whole Church and each of her parts) would require, of course, a more thorough treatment than this short essay can provide. We can only contribute a few observations to the subject. The proposition that the pope is pope insofar as he is head of the episcopal college, is, first of all, certainly correct, at least in the sense that, on the one hand, this episcopal college, although (because) *iuris divini,* cannot be conceived without the pope as its head and, on the other hand, the pope would not be pope of this concrete Church as *de facto* founded by Christ if the episcopal college did not exist or if the pope did not recognize it as such. It is also clear and beyond dispute that *if* the pope possesses his universal powers for the whole Church *qua* head of the episcopal college, he has this power from God and not from that college, and that therefore even in the supposition aforesaid, the actual competence of the pope as head of the episcopal college and so the concrete nature of his "presidency" in the college (which the above mentioned papal powers over the whole Church include) is *iuris divini,* given to him by Christ in Peter. The question is therefore only whether the conditional proposition suggested above corresponds to a reality

[19] J. Salaverri (*Sacrae Theol. Summa* I[4], p. 714ff., n. 645–648). We cannot enter into this question, though it too would show that to assume two different subjects of the ordinary or extraordinary magisterium would always lead to a dilemma.

or not. Which means: Is the relationship between the two papal functions to be understood formally as one of mutual inclusion (though, of course, only by divine positive institution) so that it is in the strictest of senses true to say: The pope is pope (supreme and immediate pastor of the whole Church) precisely *insofar* as he is head of the college of bishops; or do these two functions only by way of addition make up the full power of the pope? Is it only true that his position as supreme pastor over the Church implies his position in the episcopal college, or is the reverse also true?

Obviously the scope for serious dispute has been very much reduced. It seems to us that the remaining problem can be solved by assuming a reciprocal inclusion or mutual implication of both sides of the papal power (as we have, more or less, implicitly done in the preceding discussion). The reason is the following. If there were two wholly different powers ("adequately distinct", even if indissolubly bound together), then the pope would have to possess his (supreme, unrestricted) jurisdiction over the whole Church precisely in the same way[20] over the bishops as over other officials in the Church, or his jurisdictional primacy could not be called simply unrestricted.[21] The former is not true, because the primacy of jurisdiction is restricted by the *ius divinum* of the episcopacy, whose powers are not a participation in the papal power. The latter cannot be true, because this

---

[20] Please note this qualification. The pope obviously has powers of jurisdiction over the bishops.

[21] Of course this power is restricted in many respects, as is any power granted to a human being. The question is only whether or not it is limited in its own dimension and in its own nature by another *legal* authority adequately distinct from it. If not, then it is "unrestricted".

potestas is called *"plena"*. This is the dilemma one confronts in conceiving the two papal powers as adequately distinct. The one power is limited from outside by the "restrictedness" of the other[22] and can no longer be called "full", unlimited. But if the two papal powers are considered from the very beginning as two aspects of one and the same power, or as two concepts that formally include each other (as they are intended and exist in the present order of things), then the difficulty disappears. The pope's full jurisdiction over the whole Church and over all her members is precisely what is meant by "head of the college of bishops"[23] translated into concrete terms. And because this power is intrinsically implied in the concept of "being head of the college of bishops", it is not really limited through that inner "restrictedness" or, better, precise determination involved in the function of being head of the college of bishops.

[22] That is, by the "restrictedness" which, given a college, comes from the very nature of its function and therefore, in itself and in relation to this function, cannot really be called a restrictedness. Cf. footnote 2. But such a "restricted" function can quite definitely imply a genuine restriction for another power, if this other power is distinct from it and not intrinsically limited in the manner of the former.

[23] "Head of the episcopal college", that is, as found in the concrete order of things. The actual papal powers cannot, of course, be deduced from the abstract formal concept of "head of a society's ruling college" alone. To show whence and how these actual powers become recognized as such (Peter as the rock of the Church, as keeper of the keys, as "support of his brethren", as shepherd of the whole flock) in the context of the whole concrete historical evolution of the Church's understanding of herself, is not our task here. Here we have only to show how the two papal powers can be recognized as mutually inclusive. And this knowledge can be got otherwise than by deducing the one power from the abstract concept of the other. We can arrive at this knowledge even if no such deduction is possible.

By this brief sketch of one argument, we do not suggest that no other arguments (perhaps more essential and pertinent) exist in favour of our view. But the above must suffice for the present.

d) "Para-Canonical" Influence of the Episcopate

Although (and because) what we have said under (a) is valid, we must be careful not to demand as a condition for the truth of our thesis, that there must be systematic, written legislation according to which the permanent co-operation of the whole episcopate in the government of the Church ought to be effected. There is no need for this simply because such legislation, the observance of which would be enforceable, would, if considered necessary, again presuppose that there could be a separate authority to control the conduct of individual bishops or the whole college, distinct from the pope or the college, and compatible with their rights and duties. Or it would presuppose that the individual persons who make up the college were vested with sovereign rights and duties outside and independently of the college, or that the college of bishops were, independent of the pope, a college with rights and powers, which could sit in judgment on the manner in which the pope respected these rights.[24] On the other hand, it would be an error to think that the whole episcopate as a college does not *de facto* rule the Church because there are no (or almost no) regulations in canon law

---

[24] We must also clearly note that for the same reason there are no material legal norms in canon law (cn. 218–221) which would really regulate the functions of the pope as such, except for the general formal norm that he has supreme authority in the Church and is subject to no other authority on earth.

according to which this government might be conducted. For first of all, if what we have said about the relation of the pope to the episcopal college is true, that is, that he is, in the first place, pope *insofar* as he is head of the college, then the college rules in the pope. (Anyone who feels that this is a subterfuge only shows that he has not grasped the basic unity of the bishops hierarchically united in the pope, outside of which unity neither pope nor college of bishops can formally exist as such.)

We should add that there are a thousand ways and means (which have always been efficacious) for the individual bishops in the college of bishops to influence the college itself and the pope, and thereby the government of the whole Church. It has never been true, not only because it is physically and psychologically impossible but also because it cannot lawfully be so, that the pope so rules the Church that impulses, directives and creative ideas only descend from the head, who in turn is inspired only by God. This is false, not only because of the "charismatic" structure of the Church, in virtue of which the charismatic impulses, as Pius XII explicitly stressed, originate at points freely chosen by the sovereign grace of God, and relatively seldom with the pope himself.[25]

Even within the hierarchical structure of the Church there is a constant give and take between pope and bishops. Never has a pope based any doctrinal judgment, preliminary or definitive, solely upon the teachings of earlier popes. The one solemn definition pronounced by a pope since the Vatican Council followed only after consultation with the entire episcopate. The permanent contact of the primacy with the universal episcopate,

[25] Cf. Karl Rahner, *Das Dynamische in der Kirche* (Freiburg, ²1958), p. 43–52.

though canonically it appears to have been established so that the pope can govern the individual bishops, also provides for the constant co-operation of the universal episcopate in the government of the Church, by example, suggestions, complaints, petitions, etc. – direct influence on the centre of the Church, and for indirect influence through the initiative of the individual bishop in his own diocese.

Though this influence "from below", from periphery to centre, may be acceptable to the pope and affect his government only on "moral" grounds (reason, fairness, sympathy, charity, forebearance, consideration for particular wishes and peculiarities, etc.), yet in such forms and ways the para-canonical but truly abiding right of the universal episcopate to rule the Church with and under the pope, is brought to bear. This right (and duty) is not the mere sum of the rights of the individual bishops in their own dioceses, though it may be realized in practice to a great extent through the individual bishop's right to govern his own diocese and the influence he thereby automatically exercises on the universal Church. If the right of the episcopate in the government of the universal Church cannot be adequately incorporated in a set of laws governing the relations of the individual members of the college with one another – that is, practically, between pope and individual bishops or even between pope and the rest of the episcopate, it does not by any means follow that some such individual, detailed regulations, of a more or less legal character, are not possible or desirable in addition to what we already have. Rules for conciliar procedure, which the pope issues alone[26] or with the express consent of the rest

[26] If the pope "alone" issues these procedural rules, he acts *as* pope, as head of the college of bishops which is in tacit agreement with him, an

103

of the council, are an example of such canonical regulations. But before we proceed further in this direction, we must consider another matter.

e) Why a "College" to Rule the Church?

If we ask why the Church has, by the will of Christ, a collegiate head in the above sense there are several possible answers, not necessarily mutually exclusive. We are dealing with a free act of the Church's Founder, and such a disposition may achieve many objects through a single decision or ordinance, especially if the institution he chooses to found (a college) has already existed elsewhere in theory and practice and therefore already has various traditional connotations. One can deduce the unity of primacy and episcopate from the idea of "communion".[27] One can start from the notion of apostolic succession, as J. Ratzinger does with considerable historical and speculative perspicacity.[28] One can also take the biblical notion of a body of many witnesses, and attack the problem from a "theology of the word", as H. Schauf attempts to do.[29] Such attempts need

agreement which through the assistance of the Holy Ghost can never fail him but will always exist (at least in a sufficient degree), even though the proof of this is no evident criterion whereby a third party could judge whether the pope has acted as head of the college of bishops. And conversely, the express consent of the college can only have a legal significance in the Church insofar as the college is constituted under the pope and not as an entity distinct from him and capable of independent action. Express consent (or the request for it) may, however, in a given situation, be morally, though not legally, imperative. Cf. section 7 below.

[27] As I have done in the first part of this work.

[28] In Part Two of this book.

[29] H. Schauf, *De Corpore Christi mystico* (Freiburg, 1959), p. 298–310.

not contradict one another. The idea of a college undoubtedly contains, inasmuch as it implies not a simple unity but a unity of many, the conviction that the Church, without prejudice to her unity, is rightly a diversity. This pluralism is thus not simply a feature which is later supplanted by unity, but is something which is to remain and to which we should aspire. And obviously not only in the sense that the Church is composed of many members numerically distinct from each other. The members are to be qualitatively distinct, and not merely through characteristics not pertinent to their membership as such,[30] but also through those which are important in and for the Church. The Church is to be constituted not simply of many members but of qualitatively different members. The variety is not only an irreducible fact but something to be cherished. The unity of the Church as a whole demands, of course, a certain homogeneity among her members, which is either presupposed, or when lacking must be created. It will always have to be preserved and defended against pluralistic tendencies incompatible with unity. But even though unity as well as a certain equality among the members is the object of the hierarchy's solicitude, yet pluralism in the Church is not merely something unavoidable or something to be overcome, but something requiring encouragement and protection. This follows simply from the Pauline teaching on the Body of Christ with its many members and their different spiritual gifts, which cannot all be realized in one and the same member.

This legitimate and necessary pluralism in the Church is not only a pluralism of the individual members, but also of the larger

[30] Provided that there could be such characteristics, which is doubtful, since the whole man in all his dimensions is to be saved.

groups, of local Churches, of countries and peoples, especially since these too, as such, have a "vocation" to the light of the Gospel. It would thus be preposterous to think, for example, that the existence of the Uniate Churches of the East, with their non-Latin rites, their own ecclesiastical law and theology, their own spirituality and piety, etc. is only tolerated by an indulgent Rome, as though Rome, for purely tactical reasons, had resigned itself to the virtually inevitable, as though an absolute uniformity of law, liturgy, etc. were really the ideal. Such a theory, if taken seriously, would be outright heresy. Obviously it is impossible to lay down once and for all exact, material norms for the proper proportion between necessary homogeneity and pluralism *iuris divini*. But in principle the Church also has the right and duty to encourage and to develop a genuine pluralism in all spheres of her existence and activity, in the manner appropriate to each sphere.

Neither in practice nor ideally is the Church a systematically administered unitary state.[31] Such a uniformity has never existed in the Church, even in the Latin Church. Even in the Roman, Western Church there has always been a pluralism in every sphere of liturgy, piety, theology, law (which is not simply identical with a Code of Canon Law), and the cure of souls, etc. If homogeneity is relatively strong here, the fact is to be explained less from the nature of the Church than from the

[31] Such a consideration is important, for example in the question of the conditions under which Protestant communities could and must be granted communion with the Roman Church. We cannot make it our aim to eradicate from such communities the whole history of Protestant Christianity, which after all was not illegitimate in every respect. To aspire to this, as a single, fundamental principle, would contradict the doctrine of the necessary pluralism in the Church.

106

historical origin and character of Western culture; and other imponderable factors are involved, such as the absent influence of the Eastern Church; the schism in Western Christianity, which forced or sometimes misled the Church to consider a militant uniformity necessary or unavoidable; a certain tendency of the Roman mind towards legal standardization, etc. At any rate, the present large measure of homogeneity does not mean that this is the ideal, or that it is not legitimate to allow or aspire to a greater pluralism even in the Latin part of the Church. (Here would be the historical and theological context for the contribution of Protestant Christianity to the plenitude of the Church were it to return, wholly or in part, to the household of the common Father.)

The significance of the college of bishops can also be seen from this point of view. Collegiate government of the Church ensures that the pluralism of divine right in the Church also becomes manifest in her head, and is valid and active there. If the Tribes of Israel as such were part of the very fabric of the "people of the covenant", and thus had a permanent significance (each in its own way, in distinction from the others; for example, the tribe of Levi); if the apostles in the college represent the tribes of the new "people of God" (though not according to the flesh, but according to the various charismata) then it becomes quite clear that the collegiate character of the Church's government derives from her permanent pluralism and is destined to serve it.

All this explains why the college of bishops, even though its unity is naturally prior to the individual bishops, does not (like the college of cardinals resident in Rome) remain assembled in one place (practically speaking, in Rome, as a sort of *pres-*

byterium for the pope), but is normally dispersed throughout the world. Only thus can it actually serve the pluralism necessary in the Church. The bishops are "local ordinaries" not merely because the pope for practical reasons needs administrative officials in various places for his personal rule of the Church (the purpose of apostolic vicars and prefects) but because a bishop can fulfil the function which he has in the college of bishops and indeed for the universal Church,[32] only when he authoritatively represents a particular member of the universal Church,[33] in which the differentiation from other members of the Church intended by the Spirit can really exist.[34]

[32] Thus M. Schmaus says quite correctly (*Lexikon für Theologie und Kirche* II[2], col. 492 and 493): The bishops "represent each in his own diocese the universal Church... It follows from the unity of the episcopate with the pope, that the bishops have, in a certain sense, a responsibility for the universal Church, over and above the territory of their own diocese." Schmaus does not necessarily contradict the opinion given here when he derives the function of the individual bishop for the universal Church from his unity with the pope. This unity with the pope is founded precisely on the unity of the college of bishops with the pope, just as the apostolic college may be understood only in its unity with the Petrine office, from which it receives its entire juridical structure.

[33] That this aspect could not be clearly seen in the apostolic college is a consequence of the small geographical size of the apostolic Church. But even in the apostolic age Paul and Barnabas felt they were representatives of the communities they founded and of their spirit vis-à-vis the mother community in Jerusalem and Peter and the original apostles.

[34] This should also make it clear that not only members who are distinguishable territorially can have this function, but also members who are only personally distinguishable. The highest superior of an exempt order can, for example, be an "ordinary" in the full canonical sense, and it is thus quite reasonable that he belongs to a general council as a member.

6. Conclusions from the Nature of the Episcopate

Finally I shall only attempt to say something about the feasibility of working out certain "rules" (without prejudice to the basic impossibility of an adequate material delimitation of the respective rights of the "primacy" and the "episcopate") for their relationship in practice, which either flow directly from the relationship or appear germane and desirable in its light.

a) The *ius divinum* of the Individual Bishop

First, some consequences from the legitimate pluralism in the Church. This pluralism not only forbids the suppression of the rights of the episcopate as a whole, since they are of divine right, or such a curtailment of the rights of the individual bishop[35] as, imposed on all individual bishops, would in practice subvert the essence of the episcopate *iuris divini,* and reduce the bishops to subordinate officials of the pope. It also implies that the rights of a bishop, as the concrete representation of and the *sine qua non* for this legitimate pluralism, are a reality in the Church which must be positively protected and fostered, even by the pope. In discussing the balance to be struck in the Church between furthering unity through homogeneity and encouraging pluralism through a self-reliant episcopate, the juridical notion of "presumption" is out of place. Thus it will be well to avoid saying that the "proper rights" of the bishop should be "presumed" and the right of the pope must be

---

[35] Without prejudice to what was said above, to the effect that the rights (in relation to the Holy See) of the episcopate must not be identified with those of the individual bishop, and therefore a restriction of the rights of an individual bishop can be legitimate, whereas it would not be if extended to the episcopate as a whole.

"proved" (if only in the pope's own conscience, and recognizing that even here the pope has the necessary competence). For both these realities which have to be protected, the unity and the pluralism, are equally fundamental,[36] and depend on one another. By the same token it would be wrong to describe as "subsidiary" the pope's power of intervening in favour of homogeneity, because it is also the duty of the individual bishop himself as a member of the universal episcopate, to promote Church unity and the homogeneity which it requires.[37] But it is clear nonetheless that each bishop should be left scope for the independent initiative necessary for his diocese to be a member with a character of its own, not simply in the Church, but for the Church as well. Only if the bishop, too, shows himself receptive to the sort of initiative that can arise in the Church even without a *Motu Proprio* from Rome, only if he is willing to take such initiative himself, if he notices and takes up questions not already answered by higher authority, if he has the ingenuous courage (like, say, Cardinal Suhard) to write a pastoral letter worthy to be an encyclical, and only if the necessary scope is allowed for the play of such initiative, can a bishop fully implement his office

[36] And ultimately guaranteed in their unity and mutual compatibility by a principle superior to law, which is the power of the Spirit in the Church.

[37] By the same token it is better to avoid talk of a "decentralization". For this notion means, in itself, nothing more than a technical administrative measure, that can also be applied in a totalitarian state, and thus has nothing to do with what we mean here, which is the essential and original pluralism of the Church. A certain decentralization can occur in the Church at most as the by-product of a conscious grasp of the genuinely Catholic principle of pluralism. Hence the pluralism of the rights of various supernatural gifts in the Church has nothing to do with "democratism".

110

within his own diocese for the good of the whole Church. When a bishop, by setting some example, by taking some initiative, by posing a new theological question yet to be formulated, by enacting legislation which serves as a model for other dioceses, by developing new ways of preaching the Gospel, does something destined to enrich the whole Church (were it only by a sort of unobtrusive spiritual osmosis), then this is not presumption or exceeding his competence, but a part of exercising his office and his duty.

Because of the legitimate and necessary pluralism in the Church, the same holds true when a bishop's words, acts or legislation cannot serve as a norm for other parts of the Church, but yet are recommended or required in the concrete situation of his Church (diocese) as in keeping with the principles of the Church and the urging of the Spirit. The correctness of an action is not always and in principle to be judged according to whether it could serve as a norm for the whole Church. It may well be that a bishop has the right and duty to use all legitimate means available to him, without contenting himself with the higher wisdom of Rome or the alleged necessity of uniform legislation, to win (through dispensation, indult and so on) a place within the law for some special ordinance in his diocese. Were he to refuse to do this on principle, he would be denying that the Church should be made up of different members, and implicitly asserting that his Church should be nothing but an absolutely uniform administrative area in an absolutely homogeneous religious "unitary state".

We always strive in practice, of course, to preserve the special character of the individual member Church. But it would perhaps be well to translate this practice into a more explicit

111

principle. For in this way the practice itself will be supported at episcopal and again at papal level. The truth will stand out more clearly and resolutely in the consciousness of the Church that the intention of the Church's government can never be to strive only for the maximum of uniformity, or to consider all differences merely as "necessary evils" or variations irrelevant to religion. No, the charismata of the Spirit himself are varied. And this variety can work itself out territorially (in religious life, in the liturgy,[38] in theology, in modes of conventual life, in Christian education, etc.). The bishops can and should be the guardians of all this, today more than ever because of a certain paradoxical phenomenon to be observed simultaneously in the world and in the Church. A unity unknown before our century exists both in the world (because of the inter-relation in culture and power in the historical and political spheres, which no longer allows the existence of isolated national histories) and in the Church (in which the principle of the unity embodied in the

[38] This reference does not contradict the Church's legislation (CJC can. 1257) according to which the Holy See has reserved to itself the legislation over liturgy for the Latin Church. For (apart from the fact that such a juridical norm is not in principle unchangeable) this norm does not mean that Rome has really reserved to itself the regulation of everything "liturgical" in the *theological* sense. An afternoon devotion ordered by the bishop and conducted according to the diocesan prayer book, a procession carried out according to episcopal instruction, etc. are, in a theological sense, very much Catholic liturgy without Rome's really having reserved to itself the regulation of such services. Even if by a certain legalistic formalism the name "liturgy" is often reserved for those parts of the Church's divine service which are regulated from Rome and the regulation of which Rome has actually reserved to itself, without its being always evident that these parts are more important than those the control of which is left to the bishops.

Church has found its absolute dogmatic and juridical expression in the definition of the First Vatican Council).

At the same time, however, the differences within these unities have not diminished but increased, whether one regards these as "still extant", or as something that ought to have a permanent existence. For in the world, first of all, the consciousness of the varieties of national culture, of economic differences etc., has been sharpened precisely because of the influence of the one world culture, and changed from something merely known to something deliberately chosen. The end of colonialism is a sign of this. And in that the Western Church has become a world Church, she is confronted as never before with the task of coping with pluralism, which certainly cannot be done by abolishing the latter.

The Church today contains peoples, territories, civilizations, the differences of which are much greater, even within the life of the Church, than has ever been the case before in the Church. That these differences have so far remained para-canonical and para-liturgical, and can therefore escape the notice of the naïve and superficial observer, does not change the fact. The only difference in earlier times was between a Christianity in a single highly civilized area, and a Christianity among nations with less developed civilizations. Today for the first time a Christianity is needed for areas historically different but culturally equal. We can today no longer afford to identify Christianity with European and North American Christianity. This same pluralism is growing relentlessly even within the old Western world, for despite our unified civilization the underlying differences are awakening to clearer consciousness and more deliberate self-assertion. (Who today would really hold, for example, that it is absolutely necessary for the unity of the Church to have an ordinary Low Mass in a small parish said in Latin, and largely to exclude the most highly developed and civilized modern languages from the sacramental sphere, while in the secular sphere the growing unity of Europe and of the world is by no means due to any common uniform language, but unabashedly accepts the plurality of languages?)

The stagnation of the Asian missions among the Far Eastern civilizations, and in awakening Africa, shows (if differently in each case) that a non-Western Christianity must be developed there, or the Gospel will not advance, because its success until now (whether it wished or no) has been in large part due to the preponderance of Western civilization. In the past, this may indeed have been an instrument of supernatural providence through which the force of the Gospel could be proclaimed, but today it is a means of declining efficacy. In this situation very much will depend on whether the Church unhesitatingly and confidently opens herself to such a pluralism, or whether, out of a cautious conservatism, she decides that unity must be maintained through the maximum possible uniformity. She can accept such a pluralism with perfect equanimity. She has systematically developed the principle of unity in her law and dogma for one hundred years past, she possesses in the Holy Ghost the most potent principle of unity, and she has in the history of the early Church and in the Uniate Churches of the Middle East a ready example in her own history to show that the unity of the Church is compatible with the pluralism of the churches. An episcopate of divine right should be the embodiment and guarantor of such a pluralism, which will be the more necessary in the future (though we must hope that this will not have to be brought about forcibly by yet other iron curtains).

We might also consider whether a good deal of what is actually granted to the individual bishop and the individual diocese by way of dispensation, indult, quinquennial powers etc., should not perhaps be left to the responsibility of the bishop from the start. Little would change in the concrete practice of the Church, but it would become clearer in principle that it is hardly the business of the supreme pastor to regulate the smallest diocesan affairs himself. (Has no one, for example, ever wondered – it is quite licit to do so – that Rome herself regulates and urges such petty details as the three Hail Mary's at the end of Mass, a detail, after all, quite problematical from a liturgical standpoint?)

Even where considerations of Church unity, sound doctrine, or concern about possible undesirable repercussions in other parts of the Church require that a certain diocesan or metropolitan measure should have a preliminary authorization and clearance and cannot automatically be left to local initiative, yet this need not mean that such a regulation is acceptable only if it is appropriate for the whole Church and could be universally imposed by Rome. For example, the question concerning the restoration of the ordained diaconate (with permission to marry) which according to prevailing law falls within the exclusive competence of Rome, should not be made to depend on whether it is advisable to introduce it in all parts of the world. It would be quite sufficient if Rome cleared the way for those bishops who feel that some such thing is necessary or useful for their territory, and promulgated certain skeleton laws accordingly.[39]

[39] The practice in Roman liturgical legislation of allowing a certain feast only to those dioceses which ask for it, provides a model for what we mean here. When we consider for example, that it was in this way (that is, leaving scope for charismatic initiative from below, while the

The whole question of such a legitimate pluralism subject to episcopal initiative and direction in the Church has another possible application which should not be overlooked, the ecumenical problem. We proceed on the assumption that there exist also (not only, of course) within the Christian communities separated by the Reformation legitimate developments and realizations of Christian faith, theology, prayer etc., which in fact are not, not yet, or not so clearly, to be found in the Catholic Church in the same particular way. We proceed on the assumption that a pluralism which had a quite legitimate place within the Catholic Church (a pluralism of supernatural gifts, of ways of living the Christian life) developed, through the fault of Christians, partly outside the Catholic Church, and thus also (not only!) with partly heretical, partly schismatic distortions. If this is so, then the question of reunion must be posed otherwise today than it was in the sixteenth century. That is, the Church today is asked the question whether and how and to what extent she is willing to accept and preserve that legitimate pluralism which the separated Christians of the Reformation could (and certainly wish to) bring into the Church as legitimate and as genuinely Christian, developed in the last four centuries outside the Catholic Church. If the Catholic Church fundamentally has a real duty to affirm pluralism, one cannot, at least *a priori,* deny some such duty toward the Protestant Christians. No matter how utopian the actual prospects (judging from the attitude of the Protestant Christians themselves) for a union (in

supreme authority followed a policy of "wait and see") that the devotion to the Sacred Heart became common to the whole Church, we may certainly wonder whether such a model could not be followed more courageously in other important questions.

contradistinction to individual conversions) between Protestant communities and the Catholic Church may seem to many Catholics, we must declare such a thing possible *in principle,* for to maintain the contrary would be to deny the pluralistic principle in the Church.

Of course many serious objections can be raised against such a union between Latin and Protestant communities in the same area, (which we cannot enter into here). But at this point one ought to ask whether these questions could not be brought closer to a real solution by affording the individual bishop or the episcopate of a country greater opportunities to work towards a union which he, in accordance with his Church's situation and spiritual vigour, considers possible and compatible with the preservation of the "Latin" heritage he administers (which has of course its justification, like the Protestant tradition). It is quite possible that the spiritual vigour of a charismatically gifted bishop might prove that in this matter things are possible by the grace of God which would seem impossible from a purely bureaucratic or legislative point of view. In any case, if the situation of Christendom mortally threatened as it is today is such that everything should be done for a reunion of Christians that does not definitely contradict dogma and conscience, and all other considerations should be put aside, then here too the principle of pluralism, responsibly borne by episcopal initiative, should not be forgotten.

b) Organization of "Para-Canonical" Customs according to this Divine Right

It would perhaps be advisable and necessary, towards a canonical clarification of episcopal rights which still exist in principle and have not become paralysed in practice, (and for the preservation of the influence of the episcopate on the whole Church and of its representation of the legitimate pluralism in the Church), if we were to examine the para-canonical customs both negatively and positively in the light of the relation between primacy and episcopate. By this we mean that there is much done in the Church which is not laid down in the Code of Canon Law and which is important, negatively or positively, for the function of the episcopate in the Church. Such a para-canonical reality ought to be brought under the light of a juridical consciousness and examined to see what should be dropped and what given legal form, the object in each case being to provide the function of the episcopate with the necessary room for development, and the sure and rapid means for it to come into its own and make itself felt. Very little, for example, is laid down in legislation for the practice of the Roman Congregations in their relations with the episcopate. That can be good, since it makes for flexible accommodation to the requirements of the particular situation. But it can also have bad effects by encouraging bureaucratic routine among the Roman authorities, who in practice, if not in theory, can be tempted to regard the bishops as their subordinate officials out in the provinces.

Another (positive) example is the German Bishops' Conference.[40] It is necessary and extremely important. But according to

---

[40] Its counterpart in other countries are the annual meeting of the Hierarchy of England and Wales, the Canadien Catholic Conference or the NCWC for North American Bishops. The situation, however, is the same everywhere. The natural (and thereby also the supernatural) unity of a certain territory in the Church (larger than a diocese) seeks (though the canonical framework for it is non-existent, or exists in atrophy in the metropolitan group etc.) to take on sharper outlines, to find an

official Canon Law, it does not exist. The question might be raised whether it ought not to exist canonically as well as actually. Behind this actual institution, which is indispensable,[41] stands the para-canonical reality of the old office of Primate of Germany[42] or what was intended to be such. But if the German Bishops' Conference also existed canonically, and not merely *de facto* and with rights the existence of which can at any time be challenged, then it would be — by its very existence — a more imposing factor in the influence of the universal episcopate on the welfare of the whole Church, than a single bishop. This is not at all meant as "power politics". All that is meant is that where the episcopate itself is juridically more concretely represented through canonically unified groups, so that it can become more active, it can exercise more effectively its function of co-operating with the highest office in the Church. This does not work to the detriment of the primacy or diminish its power, but to the good of that for which the primacy exists, that is the Church.

A further example: There is no legislation in the Code about the form in which a general council should take place. At the

organ whereby it may cope with this situation and the responsibility thus entailed – a responsibility always fraught with blessing or disaster for the universal Church.

[41] There are thousands of matters in any nation which simply cannot be regulated at diocesan level, but require a uniform nation-wide solution. But there is no legal means available (except the Holy See itself, which, again, ought to be the ultimate, not the first authority for such affairs) for effecting the uniformity of such solutions for a whole country.

[42] We may leave it an open question whether such a primate (with or without the name) should be envisaged in the chairman of the Bishops' Conference, existing canonically and making decisions binding for all Germany.

last council the outlines of its procedure were laid down by the pope.[43] Would it not correspond to the nature of the episcopate and of the council (which is derived from the nature of the episcopate) if a group — its size to be more exactly determined — of the Fathers of the council were able to make additions to the council's agenda as of right, so that such proposals could not be set aside by a purely papal commission? The right of the bishops to active participation and co-operation in a council need not necessarily find concrete expression precisely in such a legal regulation of procedure. But nobody can deny that such a legal provision would be a meaningful realization of the essential function of the episcopate at a council.

If it is clear that the episcopate is not merely the pope's counsellor, when he wants and asks for counsel, but that it possesses an active function, then at least we can pose the question whether councils in regular rotation would not be a sensible arrangement. In both the ancient and modern Church the council has been, to its detriment, somewhat mystified, in contra-distinction to the ordinary magisterial and pastoral office of the Church, as if only through it (abstracting from the pope, but from him alone) there were possible a collegiate expression of the Church's supreme power, forgetting that the council is one quite particular form of the real college, which even without the council, and with another *modus procedendi,* exists continuously in the Church. Thus the impression was created that a council is essentially a very "extraordinary" and therefore rare occurrence.

[43] Cf. H. Jedin, "Die Geschäftsordnungen der beiden letzten ökumenischen Konzilien in ekklesiologischer Sicht", *Catholica* 14 (1960), p. 105–118.

If we remember that a council is certainly not called for the sole purpose of pronouncing doctrinal decisions, and if we adopt the sober but correct idea of John XXIII that a council can be important and exercise a very essential function when it acts primarily as the highest *pastoral* office, then it is not easy to see why it could not assemble at regular, though not too brief, intervals.

The late Middle Ages had this bold idea.[44] That it was not put into effect is still no proof that it was false or unrealistic. The quicker tempo of life today will certainly ensure that the themes worth discussing in a council will not be lacking (unless one makes the unfair demand that one council solve everything). And the regularity of the rotation could be an incentive not to put off urgent problems (which has certainly happened in the history of the Church) and could at the same time guard against the temptation to try to decide at one council (since it is a unique opportunity that will not soon recur) something which would be ripe only at another council. Not every council would, then, have the same rank and weight as those of Chalcedon or Trent. But such regular councils would nevertheless not find it too difficult to become as important as many other councils (*e.g.*, the Lateran Councils) which we also customarily number among the ecumenical councils.

---

[44] The Council of Constance, in its thirty-ninth session (October 9, 1417) laid down, in the first reform decree, that a general council must meet regularly every ten years. (Cf. K. J. Hefele – H. Leclerq, *Histoire des Conciles,* VII/1 [Paris, 1916] p. 459.) Whatever be thought of the motives behind this decree and the brevity of the interval, the fact that it was never carried out is no proof that it was impracticable ot that the basic idea would not suit our times.

c) The Position of Auxiliary Bishops in the Universal Episcopate

The individual bishop, according to the nature of the episcopate, is first of all a member of the college of bishops, and only because of this the ruler of a particular territory of the Church (though possession of a territory, for reasons we have indicated, may follow as a natural if, for the individual bishop, not absolutely necessary consequence). Hence it is not at all inconceivable that there are members of the college of bishops who are not rulers of a particular diocese. Even such a bishop can have duties within the whole college, can participate in the college's one task of ruling the universal Church. It cannot therefore automatically be said that every episcopal consecration that is not "relative" is self-contradictory, because it does not assign the consecrated man to a particular diocese, or that it could allot him a participation only in the *potestas ordinis* of the bishops. If then auxiliary bishops are, for example, called to the council as voting members (CJC No. 223, 2), this is (or would be) only a reasonable consequence of the nature of the episcopal office (even if not a strictly necessary one).[45] This does not, of course, justify raising those who really are and are to be only officials of the pope (a high dignity and a great office!), to the episcopate *honoris causa* as it were, to betoken their dignity (something quite unnecessary, for this dignity speaks for itself) or to enable them to exercise the episcopal *potestas ordinis*. Real auxiliary bishops for whom there is a genuine need should according to our principle be looked on in every way as members

---

[45] And perhaps not to be recommended today for purely technical reasons (that is, too many participants at the council). It is to be noted that a council can also be made up of representatives of those who themselves compose the supreme governing body in the Church.

of the one universal episcopate, the one subject of universal power in the Church, even though their rights with respect to the individual diocese essentially differ from those of the local ordinary.

d) Some Consequences for the Structure of Dioceses

Our principle would also require a bold re-thinking of the concept and actual structure of a diocese. If the bishop is primarily a member of the supreme governing body of the Church, and yet on this ground is meant to rule a particular part of the Church, and if both tasks must be intimately connected, then a diocese must be of such a size (though the ideal will necessarily be only approximately attainable) that it can fulfil within its own life all the functions of the Church (except that of representing the unity of the whole Church through the Petrine office). Its life should be such that he who guides and rules it does something which can seem to be a function of the Church as such and as a whole, an example of the life of the universal Church. This should be the criterion of reasonable size for a diocese. Where only a quite limited part of the Church's life can be lived within it, there is really no diocese in the true sense of the word.[46]

[46] Of course it must be borne in mind that because of the divinely intended pluralism, each true diocese must or may live and represent the whole life of the Church in a different way, in a different style than another diocese, without thereby either ceasing to be true to its nature or to live and mirror the whole life of the Church; and this not only in the exercise of a Bishop's power of ordination (which is always present, and is an essential factor in a diocese's realizing the whole content of the Church within its own boundaries, and thus being "Church" in the Church), but also in other vital activites of the Church. Within the diocese

It must be kept in mind that this norm of the rôle and size of a diocese is realized differently in different ages and different cultural and political circumstances. Because an "ancient" *Polis* provided an adequate foundation for and representation of the whole of the Church's life, since within the city the whole of human life at that time could come into play, each "city" could also be a diocese. This is no longer true today, since a single city can no longer sustain and represent the whole of human life, and therefore the whole of the Church's life. The central-European and extra-European conception of a diocese is therefore the correct one today, and the ancient conception, which has primarily been preserved in Italy, is obsolete. An indication of this is seen in the fact that the Church promised in the Italian Concordat to suppress Italian dioceses which were too small (though this has still not been carried out) and that in para-canonical measures (*e.g.,* the setting up of inter-diocesan provincial seminaries, etc.) the modern conception of a diocese has made itself felt even in Italy.

From this point of view, the tendency discernible here and there in central Europe to make the diocese as small as possible lacks justification. The needs which such efforts are meant to fill should and can be met in other ways (*e.g.,* by deans clothed with wider powers etc.; some old institutions, like that of the arch-priest, etc., could be renewed in accordance with the times). A diocese which cannot support its own seminary, in which (as such!) the whole life of the Church cannot to some extent shine forth (in theology, liturgy, religious orders, art etc.) is really not

the plenitude of the world ought in some way (in quality, not quantity) manage to exist, to be lived and shaped in Christian fashion, so that Church may be manifested at all.

a diocese. Certainly a German bishopric, for example, has para-canonically an entirely different function from an Italian one, and recognizing this difference does not imply that one is merely counting heads. In an Italian diocese of say 40.000 souls, there can be today (in this diocese as such!) no independent theological tradition (in a human, not specifically theological sense of the word), no independent liturgical life (even if expressed para–canonically), no conscious attitude to the intellectual and social questions of the day, etc. The material and personal basis for these things is simply too narrow. Thus such a diocese cannot really be a member of the Church with a character of its own and its own special vocation in the Church. It can only represent what exists elsewhere.

The bishop of such a diocese personally may still be extremely important in the Church (more or less charismatically, through the weight of his spiritual personality and the special character of what it represents), he can to a certain extent be the representative of a particular "member of the Church" (or rather, the representative of a particular function or structure in the organism of the Church) that is not, and need not be, based on territory.[47] Such a bishop still represents the wholeness of the Church with respect to her power of order (since the whole Church has no more power in this respect than he), but as the responsible ruler and representative of his territorial diocese, he does not represent the life and being of the whole Church to such an extent that he should for this reason necessarily belong to her supreme governing body.

[47] Such "members" of the Church exist, of course. Otherwise each exemption would lack any theological and ecclesiological foundation.

Of course, in the Church just as in the state,[48] the actual situation will at best be able to approach the ideal only asymptotically. The actual dioceses will in very different degrees realize the ideal of an independent member of the Church with its own particular calling, destined to portray the life of the whole Church in its own way, and thus provide the basis for its own ruler's membership in the supreme governing body of the whole Church and *vice versa*. But that does not make it any less important to know what a diocese really is. To see it merely as a technically necessary "administrative area" of the one (ideally homogeneous) Church is to misunderstand its nature, and willy-nilly to make the bishop in fact an official of the pope, whose business he conducts in some provincial "outpost".

e) The Office of Bishop as Service of the Universal Church

The whole question of the permanent right of the universal episcopacy (united under the pope), as the subject of the one government of the Church, has another quite different side. What a right does, after all, is to provide scope for the fulfilment of a duty. If the individual bishop is primarily member of a college which is entrusted with the care if the whole Church, if he rules his diocese precisely insofar as it is a part of the whole

[48] How differently, and to what different degrees, is, for example, the concept of a "city" realized in actual cities, even if all have the rights of a city by positive legislation. Some are really less than sizeable villages, others approximate to the nature of provinces or states. Here too there exists a legal positivism, justified because inevitable, which regards as a city any entity acknowledged as such by positive law. And yet it is possible to consider a city according to its nature, which even positive law cannot ignore. It cannot, for example, effectively make two houses into a city by positive decree. Such a positivism would cancel itself out.

Church, and if he performs his local duties as one element of his primary and total duty — then he must fulfill it in the consciousness of his responsibility for the whole Church, instead of regarding this responsibility for the whole Church as an additional and less important part of his duty. He should think about the whole Church as much as about his own diocese. He can never look on the greater good of the whole Church as detrimental to his own diocese. He can never think that his only concern is with his own diocese. His priests are not ordained for his diocese so exclusively that they, and he in them, do not also have a function for the whole Church. If, for example, the shortage of priests in Latin America is five times as acute as in North America or Europe, can a bishop say that this is indeed regrettable and that he will gladly pray for Latin America, but that nothing more can be expected of him, since he must look after his own diocese, and his duties toward the missions do not extend beyond those which all pious Christians have? Or must he feel an immediate episcopal responsibility for such lands, even if this responsibility is not legally or morally the same as for his own diocese? If such questions raise awkward legislative and moral[49] problems, this is no reason to avoid them.[50]

---

[49] May, for example, a European bishop deny an individual priest permission, if he wants to volunteer for Latin America, merely because there is also a shortage of priests in Europe? And this although those who know say that Latin America will be lost to the Church in the next thirty years, if it does not receive tens of thousands of priests from elsewhere?

[50] The co-responsibility of the bishops with the pope for the whole mission work of the Church has been stressed by Pius XI ("*Rerum ecclesiae*" of February 18, 1926; AAS 18 [1926], pp. 68 ff.) and Pius XII ("*Fidei Donum*" of April 21, 1957; AAS 49 [1957], pp. 236 ff.), though it is not

f) Concerning the Possibility of an Election of the Pope by the Whole Episcopate

From the manner in which the pope, for centuries now, has seen his role in the universal Church (both in practice and in principle), and from other considerations (some given above), it can be concluded that the Roman pope is primarily head of the Church and not just Bishop of Rome. This local office only indicates who the head of the whole Church is, it is not the reason for his headship. If one bears in mind what we have said about the existence and function of the universal episcopate in the Church, then the question arises whether it would not be most in keeping with the nature of both these institutions of divine right in the Church, if the universal episcopate were to elect the pope in some manner or other. Not as though such a thing were necessary, however,[51] nor as though this familiar idea were not sufficiently realized, in essence if not in form, in that the majority of the College of Cardinals is made up of diocesan bishops. But if the report be true that recent popes have considered altering the method of papal elections in this very sense, then it is certainly legitimate to call attention to the question here.

made clear why the duty towards the universal Church arising from their office and their "mission" is not sufficiently discharged merely by ruling their own dioceses, and why they do not simply share the missionary duty of all Christians (though in greater measure).

[51] Or that this idea should be linked with the consideration whether other nations besides the Italians might not also provide the popes. Our idea has nothing to do with such considerations and is quite compatible with the sober realization that it is best to exclude petty national jealousies from papal elections by the expedient of choosing the pope from among the Italians.

7. A Distinction: Legal and Moral Norms

In order to clarify what is to be said in this section, let us begin with a fictitious example, asking the reader to bear with its crudity for the sake of the point to be made. Imagine that the pope, as supreme pastor of the Church, issued a decree today requiring all the Uniate Churches of the Near East to give up their Oriental liturgy and adopt the Latin rite. Would the pope by such a decree overstep the limits of his supreme jurisdictional primacy, exceeding his legal competence, and would his decree therefore be legally null and void? Disregarding the question whether the pope would in fact always be hindered from publishing such a decree, for reasons which lie not in his legal jurisdictional primacy as such, but elsewhere (*e.g.,* because of the guidance of the Holy Ghost in the Church, which would prevent the pluralism that belongs to the essence of the one Church from being mortally endangered by a decree in favour of an absolute uniformism), disregarding, that is, the question whether we have proposed a hypothesis that could not be fulfilled, we would have to answer the question posed above with a clear "no".[52] The pope would not exceed the competence

[52] We must of course pass over the question whether the pope, in certain circumstances, is or can be so bound by an explicit or implicit contract entered into by the Oriental and Roman Churches at the time of their reunion, that a decree conflicting with this contract would be not only immoral, but also legally invalid as breach of contract. This question would lead in turn to the question whether a contract of the pope with another legal person in strictly ecclesiastical matters (*e.g.,* a concordat) is to be interpreted according to regular contract theory or to the theory of privileges. Depending upon that answer, the question of the legal validity of a unilateral denunciation of such an agreement by the pope, would also be susceptible of different answers.

of his jurisdictional primacy by such a decree, and the decree would be legally valid.

But we can also pose an entirely different question. Would it be morally licit for the pope to issue such a decree? Any reasonable man and any true Christian would have to answer "no". Any confessor of the pope would have to tell him that in the concrete situation of the Church today such a decree, despite its legal validity, would be subjectively and objectively an extremely grave moral offence against charity, against the unity of the Church rightly understood (which does not demand uniformity), against possible reunion of the Orthodox with the Roman Catholic Church etc., a mortal sin from which the pope could be absolved only if he revoked the decree.

From this example one can readily gather the heart of the matter. It can, of course, be worked out more fundamentally and abstractly in a theological demonstration:

1. The exercise of the papal jurisdictional primacy remains, even when it is legal, subject to moral norms, which are not necessarily satisfied merely because a given act of jurisdiction is legal. Even an act of jurisdiction which legally binds its subjects can offend against moral principles.

2. To point out and protest against the possible infringement against moral norms of an act which must respect these norms is not to deny or question the legal competence of the man possessing the jurisdiction.

3. Even if one assumes that the ultimate, most definitive acts of ecclesiastical superiors, so long as they are legal, are also practically and morally justified — that is, if one assumes that in the acts of the pope which decisively affect the good of the whole Church in absolutely essential matters, the guidance and

assistance of the Holy Ghost will prevent such acts from being, although legal, morally objectionable — nevertheless this assumption can hardly be extended to *all* acts of the pope or other ecclesiastical authorities which, though they do not formally exceed the legal competence of the concrete person holding power and thus cannot be looked on by his subjects as *legally* void, can still be disordered in reality, and therefore (at least objectively) morally wrong, and thus sinful. And this sin may not lie simply in the subjective attitude of the person performing the act, sufficient perhaps to ensure the content of the act itself, but the very content of the act may itself be morally disordered.[53]

4. If there is no court of appeal against the general jurisdictional primacy of the pope, before which a decree of this primacy could be contested and annulled against the will of the pope; if we, then, remain ultimately dependent upon the judgment and good will of the supreme pastor of the Church even in the legal sphere as such, and remain, so to speak, at his mercy, without a legal safeguard independent of him; if, in the necessary absence in this world of such a safeguard against possible abuse

---

[53] Take the case of a pope's deposing a competent and pious bishop in a diocese without any objective reason, merely in order to promote one of his relatives to the post. It could hardly be proved that such a deposition is legally invalid. There is no court of appeal before which the pope and his measure could be cited. The pope alone has the competence of competence, that is, he alone judges in the last juridical instance on earth whether in a given act he has observed those norms by which in his own view that act is to be judged. But for all the unassailable legal validity of such a measure, such a deposition would be immoral and an actual offence against the divine right of the episcopate, though not an offence extending to the proper sphere of doctrine.

of this power, we must remain trustingly dependent on the protection of the Holy Ghost, who, without such a human safeguard, will prevent abuse from destroying the essence of the Church as an institution, the embodiment of right and also of love (abuse being to a certain extent always possible, and to a certain extent indeed always present, given the sinfulness of all men); nevertheless it is not necessary to deny that there can be a right and even a duty to protest against the infraction of equity, of love, of the right of the individual, even where the legality of an act of ecclesiastical authority cannot be questioned.

What the proper forms might be for such a legitimate protest against an infraction of moral norms despite the observance of legal norms, cannot be discussed here. But in any case, the tacit view and consequent practice, according to which a disposition of an ecclesiastical superior is unobjectionable in every respect merely because it falls within his legal competence, should not prevail in the Church. Such a pernicious opinion, which definitely exists in practice, ignores the basic Catholic conviction that the sphere of law and the sphere of morality are not conterminous. Legality and morality are not identical, even in the measures of ecclesiastical superiors. Thus it is in principle quite conceivable that even papal officials, while remaining within their legal competence with respect to the bishops, might take steps within the possible legal limits of the papal jurisdictional primacy, and yet, at least objectively, act immorally. The moral impropriety of such measures might consist in restricting the rights of a bishop in a way which is legally possible, because of the papal jurisdictional primacy, yet not required by the nature of the case. Though the pope alone has the competence of competence in this matter, that is, though he alone decides, in the sphere of law, whether this restrictive measure (particular or general) is objectively justified or not, nevertheless, at the *moral* level, for the bishop to protest, much as the Epistle to the Galatians shows Paul protesting to Peter, is possible, justified and indeed in some circumstances a sacred duty. Since such objectively detrimental and thus often objectively immoral limitations of episcopal power, even by the human law of the Church cannot be considered *a priori* impossible, it cannot be maintained *a priori* that episcopal wishes regarding the arrangements of human law in the relations of the pope with the episcopate are always and necessarily irrelevant or unjustified. That is, it cannot be maintained that human law in the Church always and everywhere and in its every detail adequately corresponds to reality, that is, to the nature of the Church and to her ever changing historical situation. Nor can it be maintained that the desirable adaptations could never imply a moral duty but are always purely discretionary and not subject to moral judgment. It is also quite conceivable that such moral principles, even if they cannot yield codified legal norms, might be more exactly formulated and better adapted to the circumstances of our time and to the practical difficulties in the relationship between primacy and episcopate.

An example (if from a somewhat different sphere): If a pope wishes to issue a definition *de fide,* he is certainly not legally bound to follow any particular procedure in order to obtain moral certainty that the proposition in question is definable. Thus, for example, the definition could not be contested if he had not informed himself in the requisite manner. Nor is it denied, of course, that the pope's definition would remain infallible and binding in conscience should he not fulfil his moral duty to obtain enough information of a theological nature about the definability of the proposition in question. But neither fact prevents the pope having a moral duty thus to inform himself, nor can he dispense himself from that duty because he has the assistance of the Holy Ghost for such a definition in any case (the less so since the assistance of the Holy Ghost might operate to prevent the definition, *e.g.*, through the death of the pope, etc.). But if such a moral duty exists, then one can reasonably investigate in detail what this moral duty of the pope's involves for him in the particular circumstances of today, the present state of theology, the modern means for gathering information, the possibility of consulting the universal episcopate, etc.

Such an ethics of papal procedure in these affairs could (despite the moral variability of procedure which would still remain, and despite the incontestable legality of his actual procedure) be discussed and formulated even in public, and expressly acknowledged by the pope as the objectively valid norm for himself. Without in the least harming the position of the pope in matters of faith as an authority from whom there is no appeal to any authority on earth, such a thing might largely contribute to quieting the fears of Protestant Christians, who always suspect that the absolute magisterial primacy of the pope is an absolutely unlimited and arbitrary power, and that Catholics must at all times be prepared for new definitions at a moment's notice. It could thus be made more clear that there can well be a moral duty on the part of the pope to consult the whole Church, and that such a duty does not contradict the *"ex sese et non ex consensu Ecclesiae"* of papal infallibility. Such moral norms, which must preside over the relationship between primacy and episcopate, would of course often simply amount to rules of normal Christian charity, of courtesy, of objectivity, of respect for the personality of one's neighbour, of the obligation to consult others, of the principle of subsidiarity which does apply in the Church, even in particular cases and not simply in general. It might be thought that such moral norms were simply obvious, so that it would be pointless to formulate them anew for the context of the relations between primacy and episcopate, since they are valid generally for all human relations. That is, of course, in large part true, but still only in *part*. For it remains true that norms which in themselves and in the abstract are quite obvious are often difficult to apply in complex situations, so that it becomes necessary to work out more concrete "intermediate" norms that impress upon duller and more partisan folk what seemliness, willingness to seek advice, doing things through official channels, etc., mean concretely in particular circumstances of one sort or another.

DATE DUE